ADVANCE PRAISE

"Kirk is dynamic, powerful and fun. The audience will walk away inspired and with actions they can take immediately for more success. He creates an inspirational and energizing environment that provides attendees with tools and insights to become the agent for effective change across their organization. Kirk is very genuine and brings a lot of realism and practical thinking to his work. I'm confident that those who apply his experience-based tips will improve their performance."

—JESSE BOYER, SVP AND COO, NIHFCU

"My very first impression of Kirk Drake, when I met with him at a restaurant many years ago, was of his remarkable youth. Already the CEO of a thriving technology company, Kirk looked to me for all the world like an awkward 14-year-old who had just gone through a significant growth spurt. He was full-sized but still needed time for his body to fully catch up! It was amazing and more than a little bit funny. And then Kirk started talking—I was truly impressed.

Kirk is all about technology and "Change"—how to understand it, how to anticipate it, and how to harness it. For over 15 years, he has been at the cutting edge of technologies and trends impacting credit unions. Kirk is not just interested in what technology is doing currently—he wants to know where it is headed next.

Through his leadership of Ongoing Operations, Kirk has helped numerous credit unions understand and implement technology solutions to move their credit unions forward. Ongoing Operations' specialties include information security, cloud solutions, business continuity planning, and telecommunications. For this book, Kirk looks forward once again, to explain how digital marketing strategies are going to be critical to credit unions' success, to enable us to thrive and to compete effectively against the rise of the FinTechs.

This book promises to challenge your thinking about technology and about credit unions, and give you new insights into how we can compete effectively in the future."

—MARTIN BRELAND, PRESIDENT/CEO, TOWER FCU, DIRECTOR – NAFCU

"Kirk is an excellent speaker! He addresses topics in a unique way, transferring his knowledge with a creativity that engages his listeners."

—LORI GALL, CAO, VIZO FINANCIAL CORPORATE CU

"When it comes to playing Futurist, Kirk is a good bet for all of us in the credit union industry to listen to. He is always insightful and grounded in his significant execution experiences making him a passionate and enthusiastic speaker. One of our best!"

—PAROON CHADA, CEO, PASSAGEWAYS, LLC

"I have known Kirk for about 10 years, and he is one of the most innovative, energetic, and creative minds in the industry."

—MARK ZOOK, CEO, MAPS CU, NACUSO CHAIR

"Kirk started Ongoing Operations about the same time that SECU joined OTS (Open Technology Solutions) with two other large credit unions. Since the beginning, we have shared the same vision—that credit unions need to collaborate to gain scale and refocus ALL of their energies on their digital service strategies in order to have a chance at success. We have gone on to create S3, our second operational CUSO that frees up our focus. Through CU2.0, Kirk furthers this vision by providing a great blueprint for how credit unions can quickly engage in their digital futures with real actionable tools today."

—ROD STAATZ, PRESIDENT/CEO SECU, CUNA CHAIR

CU 2.0

A GUIDE FOR CREDIT UNIONS COMPETING IN THE DIGITAL AGE

KIRK DRAKE

LIONCREST
PUBLISHING

CU 2.0

A Guide for Credit Unions Competing in the Digital Age

ISBN   978-1-61961-678-3 *Hardcover*

978-1-61961-564-9 *Paperback*

978-1-61961-565-6 *Ebook*

Thanks to my wonderful wife, who has been supportive of all the crazy ups and downs and distractions of entrepreneurship.

CONTENTS

———

FOREWORD

BY JESSE BOYER

I first met Kirk Drake when he started his company, Ongoing Operations (OGO), and was looking for initial investors and clients. I visited the shell of what became the OGO office, but at the time, the company was only a huge, empty space with a server room and a cot next to a desk. Kirk looked extremely harried and hardworking. He was managing two jobs—a day job at the credit union and his real job: starting up his revolutionary company. My first impression of Kirk was, "Wow, here's a hardworking entrepreneur kind of guy."

My second thought was, "Maybe I should spring for a razor."

Our paths continued to cross over the next couple of years at user conferences and industry and networking events. As my credit union career took off, and I started making my mark in the industry, Kirk achieved similar success and respect from the Credit Union Service Organization (CUSO) and the private sector.

During this time, I came upon the unique position of starting a new credit union—an increasingly rare opportunity in an industry where credit unions are usually consolidated. We don't typically mess around with startups.

In 2008, I was given a great chance to start something quite new. The credit union I helped open was the first entirely branchless credit union in the world. We borrowed our playbook from ING and other online banks, looked at their successes, and launched a credit union utilizing a completely new business model.

As I started to look around the industry for trusted sources of information to help plan and implement strategies, tweak infrastructure, and keep an eye on future technologies, Kirk was one of the first people I reached out to. I became Kirk's client, and we continued to do business and grow together for the next five years.

Shortly thereafter, I became the CEO of a company that already had an established relationship with OGO, so Kirk and I continued to conduct business together, now in the private sector, partnering on a couple of products.

Coming round full circle, I currently sit in the seat Kirk sat in when I first met him in that empty office space, although that cot is no longer there. Now I am the guy in the chair, and he's the one dropping by for a visit. I've been in this position for more than a year, and there has never been a better fit for my company and for what OGO does. We're an OGO investor that drinks the Kirk Drake Kool-Aid, and my business and personal relationships with Kirk have never been stronger.

I've worked in the credit union industry for more than twenty-three years, and my experience spans both ends of the spectrum—from working for multibillion-dollar credit unions to startups. Most credit unions are still positioned as slow-growing, mid-sized organizations with many variables making business difficult, as technology changes the expectations and user experiences of our clients.

To be fair, there are external, macroeconomic reasons that can be held partially responsible for this lack of growth. Our core business model of making loans and taking in deposits isn't yielding as much revenue as it did in the past. This macro environment is the primary reason for decreases in revenue, for midsize or smaller credit unions more than for larger ones. So what are we to do? Throw up our hands?

No.

We must answer to our members and do so in a way that meets their needs and expectations, as well as grows both the community and the credit union.

As the landscape changes and the credit union world grows flatter, trying to be active in the same channels that multibillion-dollar banks compete in is impossible. How can we play with the big boys? It's difficult for a smaller company with limited funds to offer the same products and services competitively. The evolving technical landscape and the pace of change have proven a challenge in an industry that isn't known for its nimbleness.

Yes, there's a gap between what giant multibillion-dollar banks can offer their patrons in terms of services and what credit unions can offer, but there is also an education gap. Millennials (those born between 1980-2000) might know a lot about technology and the applications on their phone, but they understand little about banking and making financial decisions.

There is also a presentation gap. Members immediately pick up their phones and go to their favorite apps: Apple Music, Google, Spotify, or Pick It. Although credit unions have jumped onboard to create their own apps, consumers are quick to point out how clunky, dated, and unappealing the interfaces are—especially those for small to mid-size credit unions. Credit unions even now, in this very mobile-centric day, are still focused on trying to bring their mobile apps up to the same level of functionality and usefulness as their online apps; many remain woefully behind. Whether you like it or not, we have entered the fashion game—and we are losing.

We have to be nimble, break out of the reactive mold, and become proactive. Diligent strategic planning, understanding the digital world, partnering with companies, and innovative financial technology firms will take flexible thinking and flexible structure. This is where *CU 2.0* will help you. This book can help you lay out a road map for success.

Instead of speaking in broad platitudes or about the even broader trends in the industry, Kirk's book drills down and focuses on what you can do to catalyze change. What practical steps can you take to better position your company for success? How will you measure that success? Who are your members and how will you serve them?

The credit union industry is at a critical point. We need to start executing plans often discussed only at the high boardroom level. When it comes to our digital footprint, our ability to deliver services remotely and use data more effectively will be increasingly at risk if we're not able to provide a compelling value proposition to our target market. We run the risk of becoming an unappealing option to our current and potential members. We then also become an appealing option to someone who might want to take us over in a consolidation bid. Time is of the essence; the luxury to sit back, watch, and wait, has passed.

This book will position you for the future, and that future is like nothing you can imagine today.

—JESSE BOYER
Industry leader, technology credit union strategist,
and credit union executive voted as one of the top
100 credit union executives in the country.

PART I

THE CREDIT UNION INDUSTRY TODAY

INTRODUCTION

———

"When you stop growing you start dying."

—WILLIAM S. BURROUGHS

Credit unions have a terrific niche in the financial industry. We consistently outperform banks in earning members' trust, delivering world-class customer service, and offering the most convenient branch and ATM networks. Yet, it's no secret credit unions are falling behind in the financial industry. Forty years ago, there were about 25,000 credit unions in the United States. Today, there are approximately 6,000, and they continue to consolidate at a rapid rate.

In 2008, the US financial industry experienced the biggest crisis in recent memory. Massive banking institutions failed overnight, exposing their poor internal financial processes and outrageous risk-taking with customer assets. At the same time, the country was beset by high rates of mortgage-loan foreclosures, many carried out in a harried and unfair fashion. The subsequent credit crunch saw consumers struggling to get their banks to extend them the credit they needed, while banks raised fees.

While banks earned the ire of their customers over and over, credit unions, the most trusted and customer-oriented financial institutions, saw their market share grow by a measly 1 percent. How could this be?

Credit unions face challenges in operating under a business model that's now eighty years old. The world has changed around us. We now live in a digital economy that requires us to grow and adapt or else dwindle to irrelevance. To effectively adapt to the new economy, credit unions will have to surmount several institutional challenges: a historic hesitation to employ innovative technology; an unhealthy rigidity in governance structures; an incorrect "if we build it, they will come" approach to marketing and expansion; a general failure to understand member expectations; and an unfortunate trend of looking more and more like the banks customers hate.

The good news is that forward-looking credit unions can meet all these challenges and grow in the new digital economy. Here's why and, more importantly, how.

THE TECHNOLOGY IS AVAILABLE

Thinking about your credit union, would you say it has a digital strategy across the organization? I am not talking about purchasing an e-commerce tool here and designating an "e-commerce team" there. Patchy, non-integrated e-commerce toolkits are nothing more than Band-Aids. To truly reap the benefits of the many technological tools available right now, credit unions need to embrace an e-commerce *mindset,* using digital tools in all departments, delivery channels, and member-facing operations. Digital isn't just a channel; it is a way of creating data-driven, repeatable experiences that educate, differentiate, excite, and advocate for our members.

While credit unions struggle to make sense of innovative technology in the context of an industry historically (and by virtue of regulation) focused on risk mitigation, digital startups are littering the growing "FinTech" (financial technology) field. These new businesses are innovating and leveraging existing infrastructures, technology, and business models to profitably slice off the legacy credit-union business that can be improved with technology.

By way of analogy, let's say credit unions are the financial-industry equivalent of a high-end restaurant. In the business of selling food, we make our own bread, build brick and mortar establishments, have a takeout business, take reservations over the phone, provide valet parking, and must clear the tables three to four times a night to make a profit. Continuing the analogy, imagine that disruptive new food trucks begin to use portable restaurants and innovative technology to break into the market. They start by showing up once a week, stealing a few customers. As they gain an audience, they use digital technology like Twitter and Facebook to let their customers know when and where they will be. Eventually, they establish a regular schedule and may even expand into brick and mortar, use Open Table, and have maximized the customer mix, location, and capital equation for a small investment, while simultaneously disrupting the legacy establishment. Ultimately, food trucks have slowly eroded the profit margin and value proposition of the traditional restaurant, forcing it to rethink everything.

Now consider that today's disruptive FinTech companies are taking advantage of a whole technology menu, much of which credit unions have shunned to date. These FinTech companies are leveraging cloud technology, payment rails, mobile phone technology, and capital to efficiently become specialists in discrete businesses that are part of credit unions' traditional business model. With the efficiency and agility of technology and specialization, and utilizing tools such as data analytics, content marketing, and social media management, our new FinTech competitors are diverting business away from credit unions in specialized segments of the emerging services marketplace.

To compete with nontraditional entrants in the financial services market, credit unions first need to adopt a "digital first" strategy. As part of this strategy, the credit union needs to deploy about ten pieces of technology, reexamine its service approaches, and integrate the digital tools into its existing processes. By leveraging existing tools, credit unions can build them into their workflow and customize them so they fit within each credit union's respective community. To test each component, you can grab technology off the virtual shelf, plug it in, and begin impacting members' service experience without a tremendous amount of effort. However, you need to outline a full strategy to avoid a constant rebuilding cycle and maximize the strategy. Starting in Chapter 3, we will show you how to do this.

RIGID GOVERNANCE STRUCTURES

Credit unions are not generally known as innovators. This has been in large part because of our regulatory and internal governance structures.

At the government level, the NCUA and various state equivalents are responsible for overseeing credit-union activities. These agencies employ buffers and controls that are intended to ensure our stability by discouraging credit-union risk-taking. In effect, NCUA policies have had a chilling effect on innovation and tend to instill in credit union leaders an attitude of uncertainty toward and disinterest in change.

Internally, most credit unions are overseen by volunteer boards of directors. These individuals are drawn from the general membership and are motivated to serve and keep the organizations they have inherited safe. Due to the nature of credit union segments, board members' professional experiences may reflect the credit union's unique segment: a credit union with a hospital chain segment may have a large proportion of doctors and medical administrators on its board; a credit union serving a large university may have a board heavy with researchers and educators; and so on. Almost universally, credit union boards do not have substantial collective experience running financial—or other—businesses. As such, they tend to take especially conservative attitudes toward change. In their well-intentioned goal of serving a credit union's existing members, board members sometimes miss the fact that growth and change (and thus some level of risk-taking) are part of maintaining a healthy institution.

At the board and executive levels, a leadership challenge is upon us. We must stop comparing our businesses with what credit unions have done in the past. Boards in particular seem to fall into a pernicious peer-analysis tar pit. If we look only at other credit unions, we are wearing blinders and may be missing the new tools and strategies our institutions need to compete with non-credit union competitors. The often-unspoken excuse—"if it ain't broke..."—needs to be turned into an opportunity. If we can broaden our views of credit unions and open our minds to change, we can push the industry forward and keep credit unions competitive.

This book does not advocate sweeping change for change's sake. Instead, I will show you how to test small-scale innovations, assess results, and rapidly build on what works. An innovative credit union working with innovative technology will go speedily through successive cycles of trying new programs and initiatives. Entrepreneurs succeed with innovation when they accept a limited risk of failure and thus complete the theory-testing cycle faster than others. In other words, entrepreneurs fail faster, learn, and move on with agility. If credit unions can embrace some level of entrepreneurship by being receptive to new ideas, becoming flexible enough to incorporate new technologies, and laying aside any institutional aversion to risk, we will empower our boards and executives to improve our institutions for our members.

STUCK IN AN "OLD SCHOOL" WAY OF THINKING

If I were to ask a credit union CEO what her members care about, I would probably hear about convenience, service, trust, and rates. In an industry comparison, credit unions outscore banks in each of these categories, yet credit unions only have eight percent market share. And following the 2008 financial crisis in which banks saw consumer trust hugely eroded, credit unions only moved the needle from 7 percent to 8 percent. So, what are we missing?

	CREDIT UNIONS	BANKS
Service (avg. satisfaction)	87 percent	79 percent
Trust	60 percent	30 percent
Convenience (ATMs)	COOP – 30,000	Largest bank – 18,000
Convenience (branches)	Shared Branching – 5,000	Largest bank – 6,000
Rates	1 to 2 percent better	

Let's think about how credit unions have traditionally gone after new business. I call it the "if we build it, they will come" mentality. Rather than proactively marketing to new business, credit unions tend to build brick-and-mortar establishments, open new branches and ATMs, and invest capital and resources in new services—all before testing the market. We do this in a misguided attempt to provide convenience that will draw members. Today, there are less costly, more expedient, and more member-friendly ways of satisfying the "convenience factor."

Many banks and some progressive credit unions employ the reverse approach to "if we build it, they will come." They have escaped the convenience-factor trap by assessing needs rather than convenience. Instead of looking at where existing members live and building more convenient locations for those members, they look to see where people remain "unbanked." They only build brick-and-mortar establishments where there is need.

To truly escape the convenience-factor trap, credit unions must create a unique brand, a unique experience, or a different way of doing business, in order to bring new members in the door without spending a lot of capital. While convenience, service, trust, and rates are important to credit union members, these are just table stakes;

without the integrated digital experience that educates, excites, and validates, the value proposition just isn't there.

We can learn a lot from industries where clients willingly go out of their way for a unique experience. Take Whole Foods, for example. People drive out of their way to buy organic food and enjoy the Whole Foods experience—and they'll even pay extra for it compared to what they would pay at a traditional grocery store. If convenience were truly the determining factor, people would always shop at the grocery store closest to their house. Whole Foods, however, worked hard to provide a shopping experience customers perceive as different from (and superior to) local grocery stores—and it succeeded. By ignoring the older, convenience-based model of expansion and looking at customer expectations, Whole Foods created a customer base of loyal patrons willing to pay more and travel further for their shopping needs.

Applied to the credit union industry, the message is that it isn't enough to do exactly what banks do and do it a little better. The credit union experience has to be compelling to draw member business, and the cost-effective way to do that is digitally.

CUSTOMER EXPECTATIONS HAVE CHANGED

If you look at the modern digital marketplace, you will find that our traditional competitors are no longer setting our members' expectations: these expectations are being set by our members' broader experience in the digital world. In other words, your members aren't comparing you with Citibank; they are comparing you to Zappos.com. Your members have been conditioned to conduct business with a virtual shopping cart in practically every industry. They self-educate, conduct business online, read reviews, and validate recommendations before purchasing a product or service. Since digital technology allows for the personalization of services, consumers expect to piece together services for themselves, because they've come to enjoy the sense of power that these choices give them.

Consider Build-A-Bear, which allows kids to custom-build their own stuffed animals. Kids who have been exposed to Build-A-Bear now expect to have the exact stuffed animal they want and are less happy with the mass-produced stuffed animals that were perfectly acceptable in the past.

Build-A-Bear completely disrupted and changed the fundamental business model of the teddy bear industry. Instead of paying for the manufacture of teddy bears and building a store to sell them a little above cost, the Build-A-Bear model uses the brick-and-mortar store to stock the raw materials and charges a premium for its customers to build their own stuffed animals. Build-A-Bear also uses data and technology at every point to enhance the experience, track inventory, and anticipate customer wants. One of my children has a Darth Vader bear in Star Wars boxer briefs that sports a recording of his grandmother's voice saying, "I love you." Talk about custom! While Warren's bear is a little odd, it is a treasured toy among other, less special ones.

The reality is that retail experiences like Zappos.com and Build-A-Bear are changing what consumers expect to experience from all industries, including financial institutions. Statistically, the number of credit unions is declining, while the number of members who use credit unions is increasing. This statistic is deceptively sunny until we know that 40 percent of credit union members end up closing their accounts within the first 100 days due to bad experiences. I first learned about the importance of creating remarkable customer experiences in The First 100 Days® from my friend Joey Coleman. His research shows that all too often, somewhere in the first 100 days, expectations are not met and customers leave. My personal experience shows that credit unions suffer from the same customer defection. The credit union experience needs to do better at meeting member expectations.

INSIDE INFORMATION

Among the retail experiences setting member expectations, recommendation engines and social media figure prominently. Businesses like Netflix and Amazon employ these tools to offer their customers inside information: their customers can see what other people buy, how a product is rated, whether there is a cheaper alternative, and how a vendor is rated.

For credit unions, it's no longer enough to say, "We have free checking accounts." The message needs to simultaneously educate and advocate. Asking a question is more powerful here: "Do you need a free checking account?" This opens the member up to a conversation and education much more effectively than a traditional marketing approach. How about, "70 percent of our consumers bought A and gave us an average rating of Y; 30 percent bought B and gave us a rating of Z." This information is critical in two ways. First, it helps drive consumers to our products. In a world of seemingly infinite choices, people don't always know what they want, so recommendations and peer pressure can help. Second, social media has a ripple effect, regardless of whether the post revealed a positive or negative experience. Negative reviews are opportunities to reach out and respond, which can win new customers if properly executed. Advocating and validating are essential to the modern digital experience.

It's critical to remember that uniqueness and customization can be disruptive. Netflix, Amazon, and many other Internet-powered companies continually anticipate what customers might be looking for. With digital data, vendors can link two items directly and immediately, communicating that customers who bought A also bought B, not only saving the customer time but also potentially increasing sales. While this limits choice somewhat, it also leaves customers believing they have been empowered to choose. Netflix uses this technology extensively, offering customers a daily panorama of films based on what they've previously watched, while Amazon narrows customization by consistently offering an "if you liked that, you might like this" menu. These features create global communities and provide inside information to customers based on consumer feedback and buying choices.

BUY LOCAL

The combination of local community engagement and member services is potent. If credit unions tie in local opportunities tailored to what members are looking for, both businesses and members win. A special rewards program paired with local stores and merchants builds a sense of community, which is a much more comfortable and dynamic environment compared to one provided by a generic credit card that offers points on something a member might not even use. Linking local businesses to credit union programs and opportunities enables you to compete on the basis of local recommendations and social media by using data to provide something differentiated, local, and homegrown, while delivering a digital and seamless member experience. I recently visited the local nursery in my neighborhood and it displayed an array of plants that were 10 percent off if customers used their Rogue FCU debit/credit card. This immediately made me want to be part of the club.

HOW THIS BOOK WILL HELP

This book is about helping credit unions—helping you—gain a 21st century competitive edge by stepping out of a 20th century mindset. This book will introduce you to the right infrastructure tools and help you stay abreast of advances in established and emergent technologies.

Although there are books out there that address pieces of the puzzle—dissecting marketing strategies and financial economic models, unpacking the credit union regulatory compliance framework, and so on—there are none that offer a road map. *CU 2.0* is, however, a comprehensive road map to help you lead with a digital strategy, tying that into your existing business processes, and enabling your institution to remain healthy, flexible, and competitive.

I'm not just going to tell you what you need to do in order to succeed; I'm going to give you practical tools and systems that you can start implementing tomorrow for immediate results.

In this book, you'll rethink who your true competitors are and what your credit union's priorities should be. This book will help you play to your strengths and be honest with yourself about where you can make the biggest impact in your members' lives. It will also help you prioritize and save time, reallocating that time properly and not squandering it on things you can't be best at. In the digital world, what's relevant to your credit union and its local membership is how your members want to be treated and what services they demand.

Through my methodology, you can take a step-by-step approach to creating a great, repeatable experience for your members, while also cultivating fierce loyalty, trust, and incredible long-term value that will allow you to compete in the new digital economy. This book covers the keys to building a better digital experience for your member through my DREAM strategy:

1. **D**ifferentiate
2. **R**ecreate and Reinforce
3. **E**ducate and Excite
4. **A**utomate
5. **M**otivate

Through DREAM, you'll be introduced to many different tools you can choose from to test and see which will make your institution more competitive. I know credit union leaders are a skeptical bunch—uncomfortable jumping right in with both feet. I get it; you want to test the market and see if your members, board, and employees are ready before you commit to running your credit unions differently. To ease anxiety, DREAM will give you digestible ways to venture into social media, content marketing, and data analytics. With small-scale tests, you can see where there are opportunities to revolutionize your credit union before making a big commitment.

All the tools, techniques, and approaches discussed within these pages have been pioneered outside of our industry. In many cases, there are examples of success within the industry as well. You can continue down the road you're on, or you can look outside the industry, learn how to create a flexible institution, and react to changes in digital technology and the competitive landscape. With this book, you don't have to reinvent the wheel; you just have to figure out how to get that wheel fully integrated into your credit union.

This book has been specifically organized to be easy to use. You can read it from beginning to end or dive in and out of chapters depending on your interests and needs. Each chapter details what is useful about a particular topic and how it integrates with the topics in other chapters. Once you understand the topic, you will be encouraged to try three to five action steps. Many chapters offer a rough estimate of how much time and effort it takes to try something. You will therefore be able to compare the effort you must expend for the results you want to achieve. You might want to try an easier strategy or a more difficult, higher-impact one. Either way, I will give you a sense of where your expectations for success should lead. Many chapters also close with case studies highlighting a credit union that deployed those tools or strategies and their results.

A BIT OF BACKGROUND

As a savvy financial executive, you are probably wondering why you should listen to me. My banking experience began more than twenty years ago when I started a high school bank at age sixteen. While in college, I worked at a local credit union, Department of Agriculture FCU, went on to work at Fiserv, and then at another credit union, NIHFCU. While serving as a member of the executive team at NIHFCU, I founded two companies to serve needs that I observed in the industry: Ongoing Operations (OGO) for disaster recovery compliance solutions, and Credit Union CTO to connect local credit union CTOs and promote learning and development.

OGO launched in 2006 as a privately held credit union service organization (CUSO) with the original mission of helping credit unions meet then-current compliance requirements for disaster recovery and business continuity. The business has evolved in scope and purpose over time to remain relevant, including a shift to cloud services when that technology became viable, direct provision of telecom services to keep pricing competitive, and IT security offerings for credit unions that need this service but can't find the relevant talent.

Through each of these cycles, I have learned to make OGO more agile and effective at performing, communicating, building engagement, cultivating trust, and deploying digital strategies. Like many credit unions, we haven't had the luxury of a huge marketing budget, so we have learned to be tactical and surgical in our methods. Many of the digital marketing and social media strategies, and other tools in this book come from what I learned at OGO.

While running OGO full-time, I saw the eventual emergence of mobile wallets in both traditional sectors (i.e., banks and credit card companies) and nontraditional ones (e.g., tech companies like Apple) and became convinced that credit unions needed to develop their own platform to stay competitive in the new payments landscape. In 2012, I linked up with Paul Fiore, the founder of Digital Insight, to found CU Wallet, which has developed a platform that allows credit unions to create unique smartphone digital experiences for their members. Whether it's researching the best deal, pulling cash out of an ATM, or paying for something, credit unions are able to use a mobile digital footprint to interact with and create value for their members beyond mobile banking.

Outside of the credit union industry, I have launched another eight businesses and continue to learn from those experiences and from all of the people I meet along the way.

This book represents lessons I have learned so far from hands-on experience, trying various techniques and approaches, and finding what works best. I hope you find this book fun and interesting, and that it becomes a resource you turn to again and again.

1

STATE OF THE INDUSTRY

Every business day, one credit union absorbs another. In the credit union industry, these are less likely to be hostile takeovers than friendly sighs of resignation. All the same, the industry has shrunk from a universe of 25,000 credit unions to one of 6,000. The reasons for individual consolidations vary but tend to fall into one of three categories: overly protective regulation of a mature industry, me-too governance, and the rise of nontraditional entrants into the market. This chapter examines these challenges and suggests ways in which we might reverse shrinkage in the industry.

THE TENSION BETWEEN REGULATORY BODIES AND CHANGE

Credit unions are regulated by the NCUA, which professes a mission to "provide, through regulation and supervision, a safe and sound credit union system, which promotes confidence in the national system of cooperative credit." The NCUA and other financial regulators such as the Federal Deposit Insurance Corporation (FDIC) were founded in the wake of the 1929 stock market crash, at a time when bank failures resulted in losses to depositors of about $1.3 billion. Of course, the NCUA's focus is on not letting credit unions fail. The absence of failure, however, is not success.

Over time, the key to healthy financial institutions has been a moderate, consistent growth rate. Some level of regulation is clearly necessary. We need look back no further than 2008 to see the hazards of banks taking on excessive risk—in that case, in the form of subprime mortgage lending and mortgage-backed securities investments. However, over-regulation risks stifle the progress and growth essential to the health of any industry. There needs to be room for innovation and change within an industry, or it will come from outside the industry instead.

With credit unions, we are starting to see market disruption from FinTech companies such as PayPal and Rocket Mortgage. While credit unions should be able to evolve and respond to the new digital marketplace, we are effectively driving through a school zone while our FinTech competitors have the benefit of an open freeway. They can raise as much capital as they need, adapt their business models as they go, use a variety of toolkits, and scale as quickly as demand rises—demand that they often create themselves. If credit unions can work with the NCUA to keep regulation from stifling healthy change, we will be closer to a level playing field with our FinTech competitors.

THE PROBLEM WITH A SAFE ENVIRONMENT

It is part of human nature that, when we feel safe, we lose some of our motivation to change and innovate. With most credit unions well capitalized (97.8 percent by the last count), our industry feels extremely safe. However, we live in a country that prides itself on self-improvement, roots for the little guy, and likes watching the big guy fail. In addition, the business cycle is faster than it has ever been. A common way to look at this is through the traditional "S" curve. The "S" curve shows a business's stages of growth, from inception through maturity and decline. What businesses strive for is a smooth, ascending "S" curve.

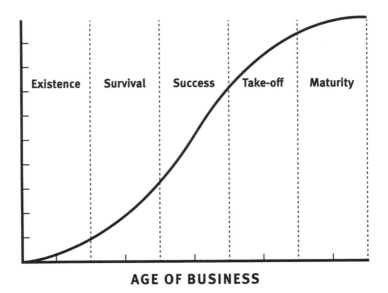

| Existence | Survival | Success | Take-off | Maturity |

AGE OF BUSINESS

For credit unions to stay out of the decline phase of the business cycle, it is essential to ditch the safety mindset and invest in and invigorate the business through new-member growth—by which I mean *right*-member growth—and new services and solutions for existing members. The right combination of these will drive membership numbers up.

In one case study, a credit union sought to create a new "S" curve by targeting millennials. This credit union had recently analyzed data on their existing members and saw that their average age was forty-plus years. These members were at a life stage in which they had switched from being net borrowers to net savers. The impact to the credit union of this membership statistic was less loan revenue, because members weren't buying big-ticket items, like homes or cars, which typically warranted loans. The credit union recognized both borrowers and savers were essential to their financial health and decided to recruit a specific new-member demographic—millennials.

The credit union sent its board reports about millennial expectations of credit unions and pitched the young demographic as an important new market, offering strategies to target them. The research helped the board understand the need for millennial members and also showed that, while millennials are perceived to be tech-savvy, they tend not to be financially literate. This meant the credit union had to tailor its approach to successfully connect with this target group. The credit union realized that before they could successfully deliver an auto loan to a millennial, they had to start with teaching their prospective member how to buy a car. By taking their member through the steps of how to buy a car, the credit union included information about how to acquire a car loan, how interest accumulates, why credit matters, and so on. The credit union was ultimately successful in employing this strategy to grow the ranks of its millennial members.

SAFETY—AND SIGNIFICANCE—IN NUMBERS

One recent example of change and innovation in the financial industry is *Chase Pay*, a digital payment platform launched by Chase Bank, which controls 10.2 percent of the financial services market, that is successfully defining a market in itself. Chase Pay already has deals with Starbucks, Walmart Pay, and LevelUp. The 6,000 credit unions remaining today only make up 8 percent of the financial industry. The top three banks each have about 10 percent market share. Individual credit unions tend to think of themselves as incapable of producing something so significant to the market, and thus, the spark of innovation finds no purchase. But if all credit unions were to adopt a technology, product, service, reward structure, dividend structure, brand, or innovation, we would have something that could significantly help the whole industry. If we could get 6,000 credit unions to put their money collectively behind one, two, or three ideas, we could create our own market without looking outside the industry. Aren't we better off disrupting the market ourselves than waiting for the outside world to do it for us?

With 6,000 credit unions on board, there's no reason why we couldn't create a tool, like PayPal, that offers differentiation or convenience for our members. The real challenge is convincing all 6,000 to support an idea at the same time. There are several examples where many credit unions have banded together and created positive change for the whole industry. I'm referring to efforts like the creation of shared branches, the credit union ATM network, credit card aggregation, and support of the Children's Miracle Network. Done right, credit unions are better together than any individual credit union is on its own.

While credit unions have a collective structure for risk management—the NCUA—we have not developed a collective structure for growth and innovation. We do not currently have a way to collectively assess needs or trends, let alone combine resources to bridge gaps in services. Imagine if every credit union signed up for an innovation fund tasked with improving the credit union experience and contributed ten cents per member per year. We'd have $10 million annually to fund and create universal products that could work with and benefit every credit union, effectively unburdening any one credit union from disproportionate investment and providing support for the innovation credit unions need to stay relevant.

MANAGEMENT CHALLENGES

Credit Unions have three macro challenges for board and management teams to manage: First, use of capital. Second, defining the competition and marketplace. Third, respecting their legacies.

SITTING ON CAPITAL

Today's credit unions sit on a lot of capital; 97.8 percent of credit unions are considered well capitalized, which equates to roughly 9 percent capital or better. Most boards see strong capital positions as evidence of their diligent exercise of their fiduciary responsibility to their members. While that can be true, holding on to too much capital is also a disservice to the members who generated it. Boards should also consider that their job is to put capital to work. They should spend the money to reinforce the bond with members through products, services, technology, or convenience. In a startup, investment capital is a call to action: Put this capital to work! Even in a financial institution, capital is only a raw ingredient. If the institution wants to generate more revenue, this ingredient must be put into action.

Let's say a credit union sits on capital and they have a 15 percent capital ratio; what's the actual benefit from that capital for members? You may have a nicer branch, maybe you have more perceived stability, or maybe there's more confidence the credit union is going to be there tomorrow, but the reality is that government-backed NCUA insurance creates that confidence. A member won't physically or tangibly feel or see the difference between a 9 percent or 15 percent capitalized credit union. However, members would certainly notice if their credit union decided to return the additional 6 percent capital to them in the form of lowering fees or interest rates, paying dividends, funding innovation, or offering more services.

DEFINING THE COMPETITION AND MARKETPLACE

Defining the competition or market is one of the biggest challenges for every business. Sometimes the competition is obvious; sometimes it is unconventional. Credit unions struggle in defining their competition, because they don't look beyond other credit unions. Credit unions compete with banks, FinTech companies, payday lenders, and outside credit card companies, among a myriad of others. In reality, credit unions compete with any product or service that helps members solve their core problems. Often these solutions can be embedded directly into a purchase decision, and the financial institution can be easily disintermediated. One great example is the effect of Uber's disruption of the taxicab industry, which significantly impaired the taxi-medallion loans that credit unions had financed.

To discover who our real competitors are, credit unions must first look at themselves and their memberships. What market are we serving? Who are these members? What services do they want? How can they be better served?

Credit unions are owned by members who have some common bond, but member profiles are usually inconsistent. A member could be a net borrower, a net saver, a baby boomer, a millennial, a single parent, a "sandwiched" middle-aged couple, a retiree, or anything in between. Success used to be measured by establishing the credit union and growing a membership. With the original leaders long retired, new leadership struggles to define the current mission and purpose. Consequently, the credit union has a hard time knowing the difference between the "right" and the "wrong" member, and often believes all members are created equal. I am not saying all members shouldn't be treated equally and fairly, but I am saying the member who gets the power of a cooperative is not equal to the member who just wants the cheapest checking account.

If we don't understand our members and their needs, we won't understand our competition. If we define our competition or market incorrectly, we can easily *think* we need to copy, replicate, and mirror whatever that competitor is doing—instead of being relevant to the real target. Credit unions need to think outside the box and identify whom they're trying to target. Southwest Airlines is a great example of a company that thought beyond their flying industry. Southwest Airlines doesn't define their competition as other airlines: it is the family car trip. Their target market is families who drive, not business travelers. Because flying with a family of four can get expensive, Southwest priced and delivered its products and services to compete with the choice of driving, creating a highly differentiated product in the process.

Because many credit unions struggle to define their market and competition, many boards resort to comparing their performance to that of other credit unions. Other credit unions may be good data points for evaluating operational metrics like call-center and branch performance, but they are a mismatch for evaluating other credit union performance aspects, such as overall growth. There are many marketplace dynamics that drive industry performance, which may vary from one credit union's market to another. These include interest rates, noninterest fee structures, and opportunities such as market growth due to employer expansion. Credit union boards should strive to evaluate their credit union's performance in the context of its individual market.

RESPECTING THEIR LEGACIES

Credit unions have commonality requirements among their membership, whether that's working for the same company, worshiping at the same church, or living in the same town.

Many credit unions were created to serve well-established companies or organizations. Such a credit union's identity can be so closely tied to the originating organization that it barely behaves like an independent cooperative financial institution. This can manifest itself in a number of ways, from refusing to rename the credit union to a failure to provide new services. Imagine your credit union was originally founded to serve Kmart employees, and many of your members are Kmart employees. But suppose your credit union has evolved to the point where you need to attract new members, including members who are not at all associated with Kmart. If all your board members came from Kmart, love Kmart, and spent their respective careers working at Kmart, what's the likelihood they're going to deviate from the Kmart brand, even when the business case is compelling for the best interests of the credit union as a whole?

Another example of a credit union charter limitation occurs when a credit union is formed to serve members in a particular geographic area. This has its own impact on innovation. A credit union formed to serve a particular community has a limited and clearly defined market. The credit union has two options for expansion in this scenario: innovate or expand the market. Both options require full board buy-in and intentional direction to capture more of the market or expand. Conventional approaches may not work, and copying other credit unions is probably not the answer.

CHANGE TO LOOK LIKE A CU, NOT A BANK

Despite losing 200 to 250 credit unions annually, membership crossed 100 million a couple of years ago. While there are fewer credit unions, the remaining ones are bigger and more successful. Credit unions are not only growing their memberships, they're growing the depth of their relationships with those members and providing better financial services. Thirty years ago, a credit union may have only offered savings accounts and auto loans. Today, credit unions offer savings, checking, money market accounts, auto loans, home equity loans, credit card loans, and full financial services like tax preparation and estate planning. Credit unions are trying to achieve a coveted spot in their members' hearts: to be every member's primary financial institution (PFI).

As they aggregate and become larger, credit unions can charge higher fees, earn more profit, and grow faster. The credit unions that tend to stick to the spirit of their original charter are often absorbed by larger ones. The local feel of the credit union, the reason many people joined in the first place, risks getting lost. The more the industry looks and acts like banks, the more consumers won't be able to tell the difference and won't care what happens to credit unions. Our best chance for continuing to help our members while making a big difference in their lives is to embrace those things that are uniquely "credit union."

United Services Automobile Association (USAA) is one of the larger mutual financial institutions that has managed to preserve this common-bond feel. USAA does a great job of building relationships with and gaining the trust of its members by treating each member as an owner. USAA also has a lot of product penetration, and, aside from providing excellent products, they're known for personal service and patronage dividends. USAA is extremely good at differentiating itself from a bank and acting in the interests of its owners.

USAA also invests in technology to continue improving member relationships. The company has been on the cutting edge of innovation, for example, by using biometrics in mobile and online banking. With this technology, USAA members no longer have to remember passwords when they interact with it. They can just take a picture of themselves or log in with a thumbprint, and a customer service representative acknowledges them immediately. While subtle, this change is important because it makes members feel like they are special—a basic human experience with a huge impact. Requiring a password doesn't feel special; it feels anonymous and impersonal.

MEMBER-DIFFERENTIATED MARKETING

Raddon Financial Group uses research to help credit unions figure out how to grow. What Raddon has preached for twenty years is to take your members and classify them "A" through "E." An "A" member is super loyal, uses many products, and makes lots of money for the credit union, whereas "E" members are cherry-pickers. They sign up for an auto loan, because it's better than their current 3 percent loan, and these members will bank hop if they see a better deal. "A" members are more profitable because they have a mortgage, a car loan, a personal loan, and a credit card with you. They bring all their business to the credit union, regardless of whether it's in their best financial interest. They're buying into the cooperative: it's better for them and better for their community. Your "A" member tends to agree philosophically with the mission of the credit union and will not rate-shop.

For a long time, the question credit unions have grappled with is how to convert "E" members to "A" members, thinking this would give credit unions the most profitable conversion. The problem is "E" members don't believe in the value of the credit union; they're simply chasing the cheapest price. Can you take someone who is a low-price shopper, convince that individual to look beyond price and instead shop on the basis of service and community loyalty? Probably not. You can't take someone who's a Republican and turn her into a Democrat overnight. Perhaps a conversion could eventually happen, but it would take a lot of time, energy, and money—things credit unions struggle with. Conversion is a futile exercise if the person doesn't understand—or care about—the credit-union value proposition.

The goal remains the same, however: trying to find and inculcate new "A" members. So how does a credit union do that? One CU focused on the user experience and eliminated tellers, which subsequently eliminated teller lines. Instead, this credit union introduced Member Experience Agents, or MEAs. The MEAs were assigned to standing pods—small, high tables with computers. Instead of sitting behind desks, when members walked in, they'd interact on the same side of the table, looking at the computer screen alongside the MEA. The point of this structural change was to make the member feel like an owner. By switching to pods and MEAs, a member was now on equal informational footing, and the MEA interacted in a more personal way, while still providing a service. Once cultivated, this feeling of ownership bears a much greater chance of shifting a member philosophically, moving them up to "A" status.

It's important to understand why your "A" members are "A" members. Why are they loyal? What are their incomes, their hobbies? What life stage are they experiencing? Did they have an experience growing up that involved a credit union? Did they acquire a loan early in life they weren't expecting? What triggered their loyalty and made them feel that tangible difference? What distinguishes them from "E" members? When you start compiling demographic information about "A" members, you begin to see how to recruit other "A" members. Like-minded people tend to group together, so when you develop an "A" profile, you can start thinking of ways to target people who fall into that category.

A LITTLE PERSPECTIVE

If you look at our history, our expansion in the 1960s and consolidation in the 2000s were driven by a perceived demand to offer more and more complex financial services, the iron fist of regulatory compliance, and a need to secure more capital. In the meantime, consumer expectations have shifted, and a more mobile workforce and transitory lifestyle have weakened community bonds. Evaporating job security and declining employee/employer trust have weakened member loyalty overall. And while smaller credit unions can claim disproportionately high levels of member loyalty, they have been challenged by a need to offer more services and a broader range of technical support in order to compete with other financial institutions. It's no wonder our industry has been consolidating. Consolidation, however, has come at a high cost.

One of credit unions' competitive advantages in the financial industry is differentiation. This occurs at a local, personal level, and it can be tough to execute when you're part of a big organization with generic products and services. As credit unions consolidate into larger, less local organizations, we must make an effort to cultivate differentiation to attract new members and keep existing members happy. Credit unions should look for ways to be hyper-relevant at a local level. This means engaging their communities digitally as well as in person via interesting, innovative, and scalable formats. Credit unions must also offer a highly personalized member experience by leveraging technology to accommodate member preferences, and customizing services and service to modern consumer appetites.

When I think about differentiation in a market of Goliaths, I am reminded of a little pharmacy in my hometown in southern Oregon. This pharmacy has been in business for seventy-five years, during which time CVS, Rite Aid, and Walgreens all appeared on the scene. This little pharmacy might have closed up shop if it had tried to compete with the chain stores on price and convenience alone. However, the owners found a way to differentiate themselves from the big chains. They kept the original pharmacy counter from the 1950s, along with a working soda foundation and soda jerk selling root beer and ice cream. The little pharmacy sells most of the same things as the big chain pharmacies do, but they found a way to offer nostalgia for older customers while creating a new experience for younger ones. This is the kind of local differentiation and community muscle-memory that keeps a little pharmacy competitive against the big guys.

A MISSED OPPORTUNITY

An individual credit union may see itself as successful in today's market by comparing itself to its credit union peers. And yet, that provincial mindset leads to missed opportunities. Looking back to the 2008 economic meltdown, it appears as if credit unions sat on their hands. If we hadn't all been comparing ourselves to each other, perhaps we could have looked at the burgeoning anti-bank sentiment and said to ourselves, "All the traditional lenders are in trouble and we have a huge advantage with our convenience, trust, and rates. Let's capitalize on it!" Perhaps we would have innovated to latch onto the additional market share that was up for grabs. That innovative push could have led to marketing dollars and different types of products and services, followed by process improvements to handle higher volumes.

That was a huge opportunity for credit unions to increase market share, but it didn't happen. If credit unions as a whole could have grown from 7 percent to 15 percent of the market, we would have become a more dominant force in pricing, service, and regulation, and touched many more members' lives.

Sometimes defining the market you are going after and the window of opportunity really helps galvanize expansion strategies. Had credit unions realized there was a limited horizon to capitalize on consumer sentiment, we might have seen that this golden hue would fade in five years.

START A CREDIT UNION TODAY: THE SIMS CREDIT UNION

If you were to recreate your credit union from scratch based on what you know today, what would it look like? Would you build or outsource your data center? Would you spend money on a physical infrastructure, training, or branding, and then let introspection guide you? I like to use this exercise for businesses in any market, because it helps me rapidly apply what I know about the current market or opportunity, without letting inertia cloud my judgment.

If you look at all the moving pieces of how you would build your credit union today, you can compare that vision to what your business actually looks like. If there are big gaps, fix them. If your credit union is executing 100 functions a day, which seven would you never do again if you didn't have to? This becomes a question of "How do I prioritize, make potentially difficult choices, and move forward?" The answer leads to practical considerations, such as how you might negotiate conversations with your employees, board, and members when you decide to stop offering a service that is a poor fit for your credit union. You might decide to let an employee go, or you might want to out-source the printing of letters and statements to a vendor who can do it cheaper, faster, and better; the list can go on.

The purpose of this exercise is to avoid sliding backward into irrelevance. You want to know who your members are and target that community, and in so doing, identify your competition. You want to stop performing tasks that are not aligned with your new goals and identify meaningful ways to measure success. The key is using technology to enable differentiation and personalization.

2

DEATH BY A THOUSAND CUTS

As credit unions continue to eye each other and banks as competition, companies like PayPal, Debtbench, and Bitcoin are creating innovative business models that slowly erode the margins of credit unions, not by competing with the entire institution, but by competing with individual components of a credit union's business. There are thousands of FinTechs entering the market that offer one or two services traditionally offered by credit unions, and when you add all of them up, they can have a huge impact on the income statement and bottom line of a financial institution.

A traditional bank's job is to loan money, keep money safe, and properly maintain a stable ecosystem, which includes transacting business, providing credit, moving money from point A to point B, and so on. What these FinTech entrepreneurs are discovering, however, is a business doesn't have to be a financial institution to offer some of these services. FinTechs are therefore finding ways of providing these services without actually being financial institutions and therefore subject to financial industry regulations. Accordingly, FinTechs can be nimbler, with lower capital requirements, take more risks, and avoid the significant compliance costs of operating as a financial institution. FinTechs are little by little taking the place of key financial services traditionally provided by banks and credit unions—payments, payroll deposits, and payday lenders, to name a few. The result is the death of the traditional banking model by a thousand cuts.

RETAIL STORED VALUE APPLICATIONS

The Starbucks app is a great example of one of these cuts. Credit unions have traditionally made money every time a member swipes their credit card at Starbucks—that is, until Starbucks launched its own application where customers can preload cash and link their Starbucks account to their phone. Instead of a member using a credit card to pay for his coffee, he now uses this app. Credit unions can still make money if the customer is preloading his Starbucks account with a credit card, which happens some of the time. But in the meantime, Starbucks has effectively created a mid-sized bank from millions of consumers' prepaid deposits—about $3 billion as of the time this book was written. That's a lot of cash deposits for a company that isn't a financial institution. If a credit union had that amount of deposits, it would be considered a big bank—in the top fifty credit unions. That credit union could lend out those deposits and make a strong interest margin.

Starbucks has managed to convince 50 million consumers to pre-buy their cups of coffee; it isn't a bank. Accordingly, Starbucks doesn't have to maintain a particular capital ratio, pay into a deposit insurance fund, or comply with other financial industry consumer protection regulations. If Starbucks went under tomorrow, the $3 billion would vanish. To be fair, most Starbucks customers have no more than $10-$30 loaded on the app. But if that $3 billion were deposited at a credit union, it would require reserves, capital, shock-testing, portfolio management, and so on.

Starbucks isn't the only retail application siphoning away deposits, either. There are thousands of similar apps set up by retailers in which people are storing small, incremental amounts. My wife, for example, has an envelope that I'd estimate has $500 of prepaid gift cards in it—stored value we either received as gifts, bought for school fundraisers, or received as credit after returning items. Collectively across our member base, these pre-paid cards and apps add up to a significant amount of money not being saved or stored in banks or credit unions.

APPLE PAY, SAMSUNG PAY, ANDROID PAY

Apple Pay, Samsung Pay, and Android Pay are three more of the thousand cuts killing credit unions' bottom lines. Each of these applications allows you to tap your phone on a POS (Point of Sale) terminal and not swipe your card. They are designed so that instead of carrying your wallet, you use your phone to pay for purchases, and all your credit cards sit on your phone digitally. The phone transmits the eventually encrypted card number to the POS terminal. As you may know, there are generally six entities making money when a customer swipes her credit card, including the merchant and the bank. Apple Pay is now a seventh in that equation. The more mouths there are to feed in this equation, the less money the credit union gets in interchange fees.

With Apple Pay, when members go to make a payment, they are looking at their Apple-branded wallet rather than their credit union-branded credit card. When members think about money and finances, instead of having an association with the credit union's brand, they have an association with Apple. In addition, Apple gains access to our members' transaction data and can begin to influence member behavior to the detriment of both the member and credit union. For example, Apple may offer their customers incentives to use their debit cards rather than their credit cards. Consumers lose in this situation because they lose credit card protection, extended warranties, and other things bundled in a credit card. Credit unions lose in this situation as well, because debit cards have less interchange or revenue than credit cards for the financial institution.

PAYPAL

Of all the FinTechs to date, PayPal has had the biggest and least-recognized impact on financial institutions. Few financial institutions today have looked at their data and asked, "How many of my members are using PayPal to make payments they could have made with a credit card? How much money is flowing and moving through the ACH (Automated Clearing House) rails?"

When a customer makes a payment via PayPal, PayPal does something called "tender steering" in which it figures out, "What is the least expensive way to do a transaction?" When payment options are presented, you'll notice that PayPal always defaults to doing an ACH to your checking account at your financial institution, or asks you if you want to use its "pay later" service. Users have to intentionally change the billing option to charge their credit cards. As it turns out, PayPal has nine separate approaches to encourage the consumer to use something other than a credit card. What PayPal does is effectively convert what started out as a credit card transaction, where they were losing money, by turning it into an ACH transaction, where they're making money.

Before PayPal, financial institutions could incent their members to use particular payment vehicles via rewards and loyalty programs; once a member enters PayPal's website, however, this is out of the credit union's hands. PayPal uses tender steering to reverse the revenue stream to the financial institution, while taking a bigger cut.

Like other FinTech incursions into credit unions' traditional businesses, one individual member effecting transactions through PayPal isn't a big deal. But what if all of your members were doing it? Well, that would become a big deal. Let's say your credit union conducts 30,000 credit card transactions per month and makes 50 cents per transaction. The credit union would earn about $15,000 per month in interchange fees. Suppose PayPal was successful in tender steering each of those transactions to ACH instead of credit cards. The credit union would not only lose the $15,000 in credit card interchange fees, but the ACH transactions would cost the credit union $1 per month. This would result in the credit union being disintermediated from the members' transactions. If you have a certain group of transactions, you can calculate the impact of PayPal on your financial institution.

To date, I've only come across two or three credit unions that have used data analytics to reveal the extent to which their transaction income has been impacted by PayPal. The last one I looked at, a $1 billion-plus credit union in the Northeast, was shocked to find their biggest source of competition wasn't a bank; it was PayPal. The credit union members did more transactions with PayPal than with the next four big banks combined!

Keep in mind the credit union isn't the only loser in PayPal's tender steering; your member loses, too. Your members probably don't realize that by using ACH instead of a credit card, they are losing the consumer protections of a credit card. If there were to be a fraudulent charge on a credit card, the member could call the credit card company to reverse the transaction and get his money back. If the member instead chooses to pay through PayPal via ACH, those protections go away. If PayPal were required to make disclosures similar to a financial institution, perhaps consumers would be able to make more informed comparisons of their tender options.

SAMPLE CREDIT UNION PAYPAL IMPACT		
	MONTHLY IMPACT	
Sample Credit Union Numbers	**Before PayPal**	**After Paypal**
Monthly Interchange	$78,450	$70,686
Total Number of Cards	20,000	20,000
Total Number of Transaction	7.7	6.93
Total Monthly Credit Transactions	154,000	138,600
Average Interchange per Transaction	0.51	0.51
Total Number of PayPal Transactions	0	15,400
Average ACH cost per Transaction	$(.05)	$(.05)
Total Monthly Credit Union Revenue	$78,450	$70,866
Total Monthly Impact	Total Change	$(7,584.00)
Total Annual Impact		$(91,008.00)
Total 3 Year Impact		$(273,024.00)
Assumptions		
*Credit Union Average Assets	$500,000,000	$500,000,000
**ROA Impact	0.19%	0.17%

VENMO

Venmo, which was purchased by PayPal, is another example of a cut to the credit union industry. Venmo has created social peer-to-peer payments. Instead of giving your friend cash or paying your babysitter with a check, you can digitally transfer payment, linked to your credit/debit rails, and then share the payment context or information with your peer group. It sounds ridiculous, but Venmo has done extremely well with millennials and the younger generations, quickly becoming a leader in peer-to-peer payments. The biggest impact on credit unions is Venmo removed the need for a traditional financial institution. For younger generations, a prepaid stored value app that allows you to transfer and pay for things without the hassle of signing up or disclosures is hugely appealing.

PAYDAY LENDERS

Payday lenders are generally perceived to be predatory businesses and not a good service for society. Their target audience is people living paycheck to paycheck who are willing to pay a premium to access their wages early. Someone might visit a payday lender and say, "I won't have my paycheck until Thursday, but I need $500 to pay my bills on Monday." The payday lender will charge a high rate to lend the $500. Payday borrowers tend to be unsophisticated consumers who do not understand the ramifications of paying a high interest rate to obtain their money early, and may not recognize they would be better off using a credit card for short-term floats than taking out these loans. Payday borrowers are thus potential credit union members who, once accustomed to banking with payday lenders, may never end up joining a credit union.

A POSTAL SERVICE BANK?

When it comes to financial services, even the United States

Postal Service (USPS) is throwing its hat into the ring. Traditionally, post offices offer basic financial transactions, like money orders, but now they're looking at offering a broader set of simple financial services. Because 25 percent of households in the U.S. don't have a traditional bank account, that means sixty to seventy million people lack a banking relationship and therefore have no established source for services such as check-cashing, peer-to-peer payments (e.g., checks), and payday lending. The USPS wants to offer money orders, prepaid gift cards, and check-cashing to this segment of the population, because it thinks it can offer these services cheaper, better, and faster than payday lenders or banks.

BITCOIN

Bitcoin is designed to be a disruptive technology to the entire financial services industry. In fact, Bitcoin takes disruption one step further than other FinTechs. It seeks to disrupt not only traditional financial services, but the currency on which it is all based. Bitcoin isn't saying, "We're going to use the U.S. dollar, and we're going to do something different with it." It's saying, "We're going to *replace* the U.S. dollar."

Bitcoin is a technology and algorithm that allows any person in the world to do business in a currency that is dictated and governed by a limited supply. It has two components. First, it's a hyper-secure digital currency that's finite, so the value goes up and fluctuates over time. Second, it allows me to pay you anonymously by validating a series of criteria without validating either of us as a person. It's a giant international exchange and, because it uses thousands of independent computers to create a public ledger, Bitcoin has no need for bank intermediaries.

Bitcoin is fascinating in theory because it prompts interesting questions, like what if financial institutions didn't have to deal with just one currency? What if the insurance fund had to address liquidity issues and a free marketplace that deals in a currency that's not based on a government, where the value of that currency can fluctuate and the government can't do anything about it?

Why would a member want to use Bitcoin? Say the member wanted to buy something in another country and avoid regulatory hurdles to international transactions. It's challenging for a credit union to process a check internationally, because onerous regulations apply. With Bitcoin, I can take $100, convert it, exchange it with anyone in the world, and not be subject to any waiting periods, record-keeping requirements, or other banking rules. In theory, someone who has limited resources or is comfortable with Bitcoin can say, "I don't want to go to a bank or credit union and have a credit report pulled, have my identity validated, and then have a trail of every transaction." Or, "I'm getting divorced, and in order to avoid paying alimony, I want my employer to pay me in Bitcoin." Once the money is received as Bitcoin, there is no possibility of tracking or garnishing wages, because the transaction cannot be validated to a specific person.

Traditionally regulated industries are required to report suspicious transactions, but Bitcoin is not subject to any such requirements. Bitcoin is constantly being pushed to meet more regulations, but there is currently no framework to regulate a digital currency. And because all Bitcoin transactions are encrypted, there's no way to track money transfers. To make matters even more complicated, Bitcoin doesn't run on a server; it runs on a social platform made up of hundreds of thousands of servers across the world. Anybody can buy a server and do what's called "mining Bitcoin," where the miner uses a computer to produce the currency in an equation. In addition, Bitcoin has a distributive ledger. Most banks have a general ledger that says, "Here are the things that happened as assets. Here are the things that happened as liabilities," and the bank keeps the final record. In Bitcoin, no individual person or institution holds the final record; everybody has the final record.

To make an analogy, a bank is like a railroad, which is precise and can travel to specific places, at specific speeds, with specific directions, etc. You know exactly what it's going to do and exactly how it's going to be used. It's highly regulated and structured, and because there's framework around it, it's extremely solid. Bitcoin, in contrast, is like an all-terrain vehicle, which has a series of rules and systems but can travel pretty much anywhere.

Bitcoin claims to be creating a more secure environment because it has encryption occurring at every transaction, and its distributive ledger is not conducive to hacking. Because its ledger is contained and validated by hundreds of thousands of Bitcoin miner nodes, all those individual servers collectively agree on the order of events within every transaction. It is therefore impossible to pollute that order, because a hacker would have to infiltrate all the different nodes in order to successfully alter anything.

Bitcoin is an entirely free market, which is appealing to some people. At the same time, there is no government or other entity standing behind the value of the currency, and accordingly, it is a risky proposition. While there is little likelihood many of our members will convert all their assets over to Bitcoin, I guarantee some of your members are moving some of their currency assets out of dollars and the credit union into Bitcoin for the reasons I outlined above. Like the Starbucks card and ApplePay, Bitcoin is just one of a thousand cuts driving down credit union fee income and interest margins.

THE FINTECH CHALLENGE

If consumer sentiment is any indication, FinTechs pose a serious challenge to traditional financial institutions. According to an Accenture survey, nearly 40 percent of North American consumers ages eighteen to thirty-four would consider switching to an online-only bank, and 30 to 40 percent would bank with a technology company that isn't a financial institution at all. While our aging credit union members aren't as likely to jump ship, even they will eventually be swayed by their kids and grandkids. Look at how quickly some other long-standing industries have been disrupted by rapid technology innovation. Do you still pay a separate long-distance bill? When did you last buy a cartridge of 32mm film or take that film to be developed? Do you go into a travel agency to book your vacations? Or, do you wait curbside in hopes a taxi will pass by? All these industries are struggling to compete with new technology that solves old problems and offers a better digital experience.

In my experience, few credit unions actively try to understand who their members are, what new technologies

or services they are using, and why. Members are us
new services that don't look or feel like a credit union. ⌐,
they don't stop to consider what benefits a credit union
might offer instead. Credit unions should be assessing
our nontraditional competition and adding products, services, and functionality that specifically targets, engages,
rewards, and helps our members avoid the unnecessary
fees, predatory practices, and other pitfalls that may come
with products marketed by nonfinancial institutions.

LIST OF FINTECH STARTUPS

Visit www.cu-2.com/FinTech to see an up-to-date list
of some of the FinTech startups that make up the thousand cuts. You'll find my database there, which classifies
each of them on whether they impact the fee income,
interest margin, or some other aspect of the credit
union ecosystem.

PART 2

—

DIFFERENTIATE

In this section, we cover the D in DREAM. Credit unions are more convenient, have better rates, more trust, better service, and great capital. So why aren't we materially moving the needle on market share?

It comes down to one major problem: digital expectations. Members today don't expect a digital experience to be like the big banks. They instead expect a digital experience that matches Amazon, Netflix, BestBuy, Uber, or Zappos. Essentially, your members' expectations are being defined by major retailers and innovative unregulated FinTech providers.

So, what's a credit union to do? The rest of the book is the guide to doing something about it. To start, we must *differentiate* with data.

The six types of data are:

1. Inbound Data (Website and Search Data)
2. Transactions and Triggers Data
3. Profitability Data
4. Design Data
5. Wallet Share and Competitive Data
6. Execution Data

3

INBOUND DATA (WEBSITE AND SEARCH DATA)

Differentiation can only be accomplished through data. Without data, you won't understand or know your member well enough to create a personalized experience. There are six levels of data analytics; most credit unions are not utilizing more than one or two of them. Data is essential to create a robust digital strategy; every chapter in this book requires some form of data to build a digital-first ecosystem.

To begin with, you need basic analytics, which will give you basic metrics and performance on your website, inbound-search, delivery channels, branches, and transaction-level information. Second, you'll need transaction and wallet-share level data so you can identify your competition and marketplace. Next, data is key for triggers. The credit union needs to build a robust ITTT("if this than that") structured library of information to know how to move the member through the experience. Fourth, profitability data is essential to making sure the credit union achieves its ROA, capital, and other goals. Combining marketplace and transactional data allows you to then create the fifth segment: data for design, in order to create new products, services, and experiences. Finally, you need execution data. This data is what ties it all together and allows you to automate the whole experience.

Let's start with basic analytics. Does your credit union have Google analytics turned on for your website? Do you know what your members are Googling? Do you have an MCIF (marketing customer information file) system? Do you know which products and members are more profitable? If not, the cheapest and easiest thing to do is to implement Google analytics. Simply create a Google account, set up an analytics key, and add the key to your website. Once this is integrated, you will begin seeing how members are finding your website, what they are doing while there, and where they go next—all of which is essential to create a repeatable experience for your members. After that, an MCIF will enable you to track and segment your members for different promotions.

Finally, a service like Raddon can help you classify and know which members, products, and services are most profitable (i.e., deliver the most value) to your members.

You might be asking, "Why do we care how or where the member is doing the transaction?" The answer is simple: you need to know when, where, why, and how the member is transacting business in order to know when, where, why, and how to educate the member and differentiate your credit union. Data analytics can be used to see how members are using the branch, ATMs, call center, and so on. Once you're utilizing the data to understand how your members are interacting, start asking appropriate questions. Is a branch profitable? If a branch isn't profitable, should you close it? Is one member service representative more efficient than another? Is the member experience better at an ATM or a kiosk? Understanding how members are interacting and how they want to interact becomes key—and data analytics starts to drive all these components.

The biggest expense in most credit unions is labor, yet few credit unions work to create metrics that incent labor efficiency and member experience. If you reduce the number of mistakes on routine transactions and the amount of time per interaction by using containerized content and self-education tools, you tend to create a consistent digital experience that values the member's—and your employees'—time, leading to consistency, efficiency, digital trust, and personalized service. When these are combined, you create a superb digital experience throughout the organization while getting more scalability.

What if you took your transactional data from the delivery channel and mashed it up with your social media data? You'll start seeing a different picture of how and why members interact, exposing delivery systems that may not be working as well as you want or ones already working extremely well.

The point of mashing up all your data points is so you can identify member patterns and behaviors and use them to guide future decisions, promotions, and actions. For example, say a member comes into a branch and asks for a cashier's check. Three days later, he returns to cancel his debit card. Three days after that, you notice his usual fifteen bill-pay items are down to ten. If you looked at these actions individually within their specific delivery channels, they may not tell you much, but if you looked at them in the aggregate and used data analytics, you can identify and compare those actions to someone who might be ticked about something and is in the process of switching financial institutions. Maybe this person is savable and an MSR could reach out and say, "Hey, we noticed you're slowly moving some business away, can you tell me more about that? Oh, our credit card limit isn't enough for you? Let's take care of this to make you happy."

Finally, once you understand the key data points about your member and the problems they will be solving, you can act on that data through transactions and triggers.

BONUS MATERIAL

Please visit www.cu-2.com/differentiate to learn how to use data more effectively in your credit union.

EASY WAYS TO TRY IT

1. Go to analytics.google.com to acquire your Google analytics tracking code.

2. Embed the code on your website.

3. Wait thirty days and then review the data and member flow from the website.

4. Review the data for page bounces—this means the member didn't find what he or she expected—and the most common places where members leave the site—these are great places to hook them back to other resources and tools.

TRANSACTIONS
AND TRIGGERS

Personalization and the four P's of marketing (price, place, product, and promotion) are key ways to deliver a properly timed micro-campaign to your member. Asking a member to refinance his mortgage three days after he completes it with a different lender isn't effective. Transactional data combined with triggers are an essential way to steer the member in a near-real-time format with highly personalized offers.

Although this transactional and social data might not matter in the banking world—and most banks are pretty bad at using it to their benefit—it does matter in the digital world and the world beyond, because of the expectations set by companies like Amazon, Uber, and Netflix. Due to the way these companies set up their user interfaces and the data they collect, they're able to create a member profile based not only on your demographic life stage, but on who you are as a person. You can't assume your members are entering a certain life stage based on age demographics alone. A twenty-two-year-old college graduate and a fifty-five-year-old widow who has to raise her grandchildren might both be entering the workforce at the same time, for example. They're both entering the same life stage, even though they're not in the same age group.

Credit unions are in a unique position to learn about their members through data analytics. We know when members move, get divorced, have kids, and start shopping somewhere new. We know when these unique life stages happen based on our data, yet most credit unions do little with this information. If we combine this information with social media data—likes and preferences around sports teams, hobbies, personal interests, etc.—we would have a much more holistic picture of our members. In addition, using their inbound data gives us key insights into the problems they are trying to solve. Combining inbound + transactions and triggers allows us to fill in the gaps and intrinsically know our members' current life stage(s). When we combine social with transaction data, we better understand who our members are, where they are in their lives, what things they're interested in, and the problems they might be experiencing.

If you see your members are using Venmo, PayPal, Bitcoin, or even payday lenders, that should tell you where your members are in their life stage, what they're trying to do, and whether they're frustrated with your institution.

The information gleaned from such transactional and social data will be different for every credit union. We spend a lot of time in this country talking about the median income in one location versus another, but that generalization has some serious flaws. I've lived in places with an extremely high median income, but the cost of housing was so expensive, I'm not sure it mattered. Those two things aren't comparable. You have to look much more acutely at your membership, your region, and other traits from a data analytics perspective to better understand the specific needs of your community and how your branch can meet them.

TOOLS AND TECHNIQUES

Credit unions shouldn't analyze data on a static basis. The problem with Experian data, Raddon, or building a marketing profile based on a point-in-time snapshot is that by the time all the information is ready for analysis, it's old. The speed at which people are moving through these environments and life stages is so rapid that if you aren't constantly revisiting the data, you and your credit union will continue to fall behind. One of the principles of marketing is, if you're not in the right place at the right time to leverage an opportunity, you'll miss it. Point-in-time snapshot data analytics are not effective. We live in a world where looking at and refreshing data constantly is a necessity. As the lives of your members change, your data changes, too. These changes should be tracked, correlated, and investigated so they can be used to create member-driven education and services using marketing automation.

Once you're analyzing these snapshots on a regular basis, how do you inject that knowledge into other delivery channels—like the call center, branches, and online banking? That's where marketing automation becomes key, because once you know those different trigger points, you can figure out when to push that information, which is important for two reasons: it allows you to hit the principles of marketing from a time, place, and purpose perspective; and it allows you to be uber-efficient with how you're spending your resources. If a member isn't ready to buy a car, spending money to market a car loan to her doesn't make sense. You're better off spending $10 to market the car loan on the right day to those interested in a car than spending $7 on the wrong day and hoping your message reaches the right audience.

Here is a quick way to test transactions and triggers, but before you get too far, we should make sure we are focused on the profitable members!

EASY WAYS TO TRY IT

1. Have your IT department run a report daily of any members who hit a transaction volume-related fee, like a fourth foreign ATM transaction, when you only give three for free.

2. Once a day, pick one member and have your call center or service center reach out and waive one fee for one member with a nicely drafted email.

3. Send a Survey Monkey survey a day later to thirty members you waived the fee for and thirty you didn't.

4. Review the data after thirty days and compare.

CASE STUDY: RANDOM CREDIT UNION

Random Credit Union was looking for growth but also wanted to gain a deep understanding of how its members were transacting business. RCU is a $1B+ credit union located in a highly competitive marketplace, was an early adopter of CU Wallet, had a website with a solid responsive web design, and implemented the early elements of a CU 2.0 strategy.

RCU used traditional data analytics technologies like Raddon (profitability data) and credit bureau data (wallet-share lite), among other approaches. Prior approaches did produce one-time results, but they didn't provide the ongoing data insights that drive short- and long-term decision-making for the credit union as well as short- and long-term value for the member. As part of a new effort, RCU tried using Nexus Intelligence to analyze wallet share and competitor data, and leverage their real-time transactions and trigger data.

The credit union saw results immediately. Within the first cut of the data, it became obvious where to focus the credit union's efforts. The most eye-opening discovery was identifying the number one competitor as PayPal, which landed ahead of the top four big banks combined (see table on the following page).

RCU immediately began working on deliberate strategies to develop products and services that compete with PayPal, as well as target those members with mobile wallets and other engaging solutions aiming to shift the member's digital impression and engagement.

Data was gathered from the core, transaction fees (payroll/ACH/share drafts) and other sources. The credit union only spent a few thousand dollars per month to perform the analysis and began incorporating data-driven decision-making throughout the organization. RCU conducted an A/B test of its normal marketing approaches to 4,000 members in group A and then used Nexus Intelligence analytics in group B. The result was 3.5 times the number of loans!

Moving forward, the credit union plans to actively develop campaigns and strategies to address the market threat and will continue to measure results.

1	Payal	11,923
2	Bank of America	10,028
3	Capital One	8,080
4	JP Morgan	7,338
5	TD Ameritrade	6,043
6	Wells Fargo	4,860
7	IC FCU	4,596
8	Santander Bank	4,490
9	Discover	4,322
10	Citibank	4,004
11	Comenity Bank	3,423
12	Digital FCU	3,378
13	Citizens Bank	3,256
14	American Express	2,773
15	Athol Saving Bank	2,772
16	Leominster Credit Union	2,720
17	Visa	2,399
18	UniBank	2,297
19	Barclays Bank	2,288
20	Synchrony Bank	2,265
21	GFA FCU	2,029
22	Fidelity Bank	2,002
23	Toyota	1,912
24	Enterprise Bank	1,797
25	Etsy Inc	1,740
26	Eclipse Cash Systems	1,731
27	US Bank	1,714
28	Intuit	1,702
29	Oreilly Auto	1,677
30	MasterCard	1,573
31	Honda	1,240
32	Credit One Bank	1,115
33	Navient	1,001
34	Venmo	983
35	Department of Education	950
36	Commerce Bank	881
37	Target Bank	855
38	Peoples United Bank	827
39	PNC Bank	761
40	Amazon	723

5

DATA ABOUT
PROFITABILITY

It is equally important in this process to understand the implications of your profitability data. Without this data, it's easy to chase a member profile or service that is highly unprofitable. Consequently, using something like Raddon—where you can ascertain which members are interested purely in price and which ones are interested in the credit union's value proposition—is extremely helpful as you design and incorporate your data into your decisions.

Many credit unions are good at this today, since they've started with these analytics a long time ago, so I won't spend time on them here.

6

DATA FOR DESIGN

———

Credit unions today don't have a good sense of who their members are because they are stuck on focusing on an "average" member, who happens to be a forty-year-old male. That average member doesn't paint a full picture of the needs of your membership or how they're interacting with the credit union. Making decisions based on the "average member" also ignores the technology credit unions have that can offer a better understanding of their membership.

In talking about how to look at these segments, Brad Powell, CEO of Axiaware, states: "Most of these generational buckets contain between twenty and eighty million people. If you have conversations with any three people, they probably will have three different approaches to work, so when you extrapolate that to fifty million people, it becomes hard to generalize."

There are, however, some safe assertions we can make about the various generations in today's workforce.

- There are three to five generations in the workplace right now; globally, that's the most there's ever been.
- That means three to five generations with earning power, and three to five generations considering banks to hold their income.
- The single-biggest difference between the oldest workers and the youngest workers (besides income level) is comfort with technology.
- While there are some from the Silent Generation (72+ years old) who can do anything on their smartphones, in general, younger generations will be more comfortable and accepting of digital and mobile.

Today, credit unions have to be hyper-focused and understand the various personas that make up their membership—the single mom, the single dad, the married couple, the single person, the retired person, the married retired couple, and so on. Each of these members is at a different life stage with various life complexities that need to be addressed individually. Assuming they're all a forty-year-old man doesn't address these complexities.

The key is using data to analyze the needs of your current members and market, and then designing specific products and services. Data is a bit of an art, so use common sense and spend some time testing before drawing any real conclusions. When you can assess key trends and data points, the credit union's ability to create a successful product is much more predictable and effective. One example from a credit union I worked at involved getting non-members to pay for our ATM deployments. We found that ATMs near food—cafeterias or sandwich shops—had three to four times the foreign card fees as our other ATMs. Over time, that became a key criteria for determining where to place an ATM, and it essentially paid for our members' convenience with non-member money!

BONUS MATERIAL

Download my suggestions on the latest and upcoming tools regarding member service technology here: www. cu-2.com.

CASE STUDY: INSPIRUS CREDIT UNION AND IQR

Collin Campbell, Vice President Strategic Initiatives, identified problems within Inspirus Credit Union and IQR, and has since leveraged big data to facilitate growth. The problem was two-fold, both related to the card portfolio. The credit union needed to introduce a card for transactors who spend every day and make projections on the new products' success. IQR therefore launched two cards—a Visa Signature rewards card and a Visa black card for the broad market, a prestigious product but also accessible with 2 percent unlimited cash back.

The other problem was the credit union didn't have quants, meaning it didn't have people to crunch and analyze data and turn it into usable and actionable items. In its first attempt, IQR was able to provide resources for quantitative, informed, and relevant credit-card experiences. IQR completed a full analysis and within a year redesigned credit tiers, types of products, pricing, and credit increases—all focused on better engaging its members across its entire card portfolio.

Although its board was not a part of the process, the amount the credit union spent was fully justified by new opportunity and revenue, according to Campbell. The results so far have been quantifiable, as the credit union has received positive feedback from its members on the quality of the cards and their features. They have also seen widespread adoption of the new products.

When asked how important this was to the credit union, Campbell said, "On a scale from one to ten: nine." He emphasized the importance of looking past thinking of this as a portfolio, and that credit unions should think about the people behind the data. Data analytics are a way to listen based on member behavior, where they are spending, how they are spending, and so on. It's invaluable information.

Moving forward, Inspirus Credit Union plans to implement marketing automation for triggers based on transactions.

7

DATA ANALYTICS FOR EXECUTION

———

Use your data to start thinking about specific member experiences and how those can be replicated throughout the environment. How do you refund an overdraft fee in distinction to how you refund a late payment fee? Is that the same in a branch? Is it the same in the call center? Is it the same through online banking? If it isn't, how does it differ in each of those environments?

This first piece is understanding all the different interactions, how they work together, and what the nuances are. Once you've containerized those, then ask about the experiences you want to prevent. If you knew a member was thinking of leaving, what would you do differently? If you knew members were gradually adding more debt and looked like they were undergoing financial stress, what would you do? Think of all the scenarios, possibilities, and questions, build containers around what you would do about them, and then put the data analytics in place to alert you when they're happening.

The next tool to implement is marketing automation in order to automatically and effectively respond to specific actions. (See Chapter 16 for more on this.) It's a multi-layered conversation you need to put together in order to use chunks of information and analytics in all the different cases in which you can drive value. Maybe a member completed fifty-eight transactions in the last six weeks and she's moved three bill-pay items over to the credit union. If you had a system that flagged her through these data points, someone from the credit union could see she clearly likes the credit union, and you could therefore follow up to ask her for more business.

Many credit unions struggle to understand the implications of data. Other credit unions have gone out and spent hundreds of thousands of dollars on data warehouses. Ultimately, the purpose of data collection and analysis is to make better decisions and gather key insights that give you a competitive advantage. Start with asking questions that steer you to be proactive.

For example, complete the following:

> If I knew which branches were profitable, I would do _____

> If I knew when a member did _____, I would do _____

> When a member does _____, it means _____

Some of my favorites are:

> If a member starts cancelling bill-pay items, it probably means they are closing their account.

> If I knew when a member sold their house, I would offer them _____.

> If a member was researching buying a new car, it would be a good time to offer a car loan.

Each of these questions enables us to gather or find existing data that supplies answers. If members start cancelling bill-pay items, they are probably planning on switching financial institutions. A call from an MEA might help keep that member engaged if the credit union was proactive in understanding why the bill-pay items were being canceled. Maybe it means the member is going through a divorce. Maybe he's unhappy with a service or the way he was treated over the phone or in person. Either way, as you start asking if/then questions, you begin gaining valuable insight about your members' behaviors. These insights are used regularly by FinTech companies to gradually move eyeballs and mindsets away from credit unions.

Consequently, there are two pieces to data analytics and service technology. The first is you need data analytics within marketing and sales automation. The second is capitalizing on the right opportunities.

You need to know how transactions are performed, why they're performed that way, what delivery channels customers are using, and, based on this, how to improve the customer experience. For example, one credit union distilled IT down to cost-per-transaction.

"Here's all the different ways a member can interact with us; here's all the costs associated with IT; here's the number of transactions and interactions they have with the credit union; and here's what it costs for that transaction."

Credit unions can do two things with that information. They can try to lower costs to provide more value, or they can try to get more transactions on top, which by default lowers costs. They can increase the numerator or decrease the denominator to build a better relationship with the member.

Let's use a credit card activation campaign as another example and compare a traditional campaign with a data-driven one.

APPROACH/STEP	TRADITIONAL DIRECT MAIL	DATA DRIVEN WITH CONTENT
Design the offer/ promotion	Create copy and design work	Have multiple offers aimed at demographic pools and specific goals (debt consolidation, balance transfer, convenience)
Print mail pieces	$$$$	Low cost
Qualify members	Gather names and mailing addresses	Use data to map which members would like which offer. For example, members who are paying five or six credit cards might be more likely to switch to a single card. Or, use the data to time the offer for convenience to the member.
Update rates and website	Update rates and website	Same, but add content explaining different reasons members switch to your credit card and why they don't. (The latter is key for not selling to the member and being trustworthy.)
Update posters	Update posters with promotion	Same
Send offer	Drop mail piece	Don't bother—spend a lot less money
Measure results	Hope for a 1 percent response rate	Much higher

In general, credit unions need to move away from a once-a-year data feed and traditional print advertising/direct mail pieces. If you want digital engagement, you have to be involved in the member's life. That means providing the right education, the right content, and the right offers. Or, in marketing terms, the product, price, and place all need to be aligned with the member.

EASY WAYS TO TRY IT

1. Have your IT department review which members have direct deposit and which ones don't.

2. Send an offer to 100 members the week before they get paid with an offer to switch their direct deposit.

3. Send an offer to 100 members within fifteen minutes of them getting paid (just time it with when your accounting department posts the morning file) with a quick switch option. Include a free cup of coffee and a T-shirt for their time.

4. Measure the results and compare.

PART 3

RECREATE AND REINFORCE

In this section, we cover the R in DREAM. To accomplish this, we must create repeatable processes that are reinforced with social media. Why? Ultimately, Google search governs much of how we interact with the world. Google favors local content that is relevant and authoritative. At the same time, most people like being well educated about their choices, so they turn to Google. The following formula is a simplified way of looking at how Google sees our credit unions, and how we can, in turn, help Google see us the way we are.

GOOGLE EQUATION

1. Credit unions know their local markets better than anyone; +

2. Credit unions know how to solve their members' problems; +

3. Credit unions can create highly educational content, and since credit unions always do the right thing, they are highly trustworthy; =

4. Google search will preference local, trustworthy, authoritative content.

CREDIT UNION EQUATION

1. Writing/video/blog content that is local, trustworthy, and educational is good for our members; +

2. Sharing that content by email (either in a bulk blast or by MSRs) increases the number of people reading the info and teaching Google about the problems our credit unions solve; +

3. Sharing our content on social media further generates interest and shows Google our knowledge; =

4. Google determines the credit union is the right local, trustworthy, and authoritative source for information for members who are searching.

    a. By product = the credit union gets a consistent process and answers.

    b. By product = the credit union gets a one-to-many approach to digital trust.

NEW MEMBER VIEW

1. Member searches for a solution to a problem
2. Google provides an answer
3. Member reads and self-educates, which builds trust
4. Member makes a decision and validates that decision on social media
5. Member opens account
6. Credit union reinforces the experience

To join our Facebook Credit Union 2.0 Group, please visit www.facebook.com/groups/creditunion2.0.

SOCIAL MEDIA RULES

Once you have begun to use data to differentiate and have created a platform that allows you to educate and exhilarate, you can then move on to validation.

Today, validation happens through social media such as Facebook and Yelp, which help people make key decisions. In the past, we might have asked our neighbors, parents, grandparents, or siblings for key referrals, but today, we trust random people online. By reading reviews and researching other people's experiences, we are exposed to a more accurate picture that tells us if the things the reviewer cares about are the same things we care about. It isn't helpful to know my father likes a particular hammer if I don't know how he uses it. Credit unions need to recreate experiences across a large number of services, products, and transactions, because if they don't, the inconsistency will come through via social validation and cause friction in your members' decisions.

Credit unions are cooperatives and, by their very definition, communities. Most credit unions, however, are bad at engaging their membership digitally or in a communal format. People have a desperate need to belong, and social media is one of the best ways to do that. Social media allows credit unions to connect, educate, share, and engage with their members, community, key influencers, and market all at once. Members want to feel part of something, and social media is a great way to enable that feeling. More importantly, it also allows them to engage on their timeline and with social validation. Social media also enables a credit union to engage its members on a one-to-many basis. The efficiency and power of this approach essentially creates a digital platform that constantly enhances the brand and value proposition for your best members.

Credit unions can use social media to drive value and experience through content. If you build an online community, it gives non-members an opportunity to learn and engage with you, potentially opening up doors to bringing in new members. Social media is an opportunity to provide information to the masses—both to your members and non-members, especially if you host contests and engage followers with useful information. Once you've built a social media following, you have an active audience to whom you can start promoting offers and special deals on financial services. What's great about social media is those who liked your page are people who are interested in you and your products, so when you're ready to host a special discount event, your message will reach a marketplace that's already interested in you, instead of you spending money trying to reach an unknown market.

Social media is a vehicle for engaging with your community, and it allows them to engage with you. Followers will talk about your credit union and share their experiences with their own followers, which opens plenty of opportunities regardless of the interaction. Some followers will share positive experiences; some will express frustrations and complain—and that's okay! Public negative experiences open up a door for your credit union to step in and fix the situation. I recommend reaching out to those who complain and turning them into secret shoppers. Jay Bear argues that you should take members who complain about your credit union, address their issues in a public sphere, and then engage them privately with a separate message saying, "I think you have some good insight about our credit union. Are you willing to be a secret shopper for us? Would you be willing to help us be a better credit union for our members?" These people almost always say yes, in which case you've taken critics and turned them into some of your most loyal, ardent fans because you invited them to be part of the solution. Most credit unions are afraid of members saying mean things about their brand online, but they shouldn't be. We have to reframe that perspective and not look at members as complainers, but look at this as an opportunity to listen to feedback to improve the member experience.

USE OF CONTENT

Marcus Sheridan, the Sales Lion, sums this up perfectly: they ask, you answer. In Chapter 12, we will cover content in greater detail. For now, we will focus on where to educate your members in the "reinforce" stage. Credit unions need to create content that's going to educate their members and encourage them to continue doing business. Perhaps it's an article on the best place to acquire a car loan, the best types of car loans, what the difference between a two-year and a five-year car loan is, and why readers would want one over the other. All these are examples of questions your members might have about a particular product, service, or life-stage event. If your credit union is the one to provide the answers to these questions, your members will find more value in you.

Once you have that content, the way you make this even more local and more effective is to use Google to your advantage. What do people do nowadays when they have a question? They Google it. When someone uses Google to ask for a service your credit union excels at, you want to make sure the answer to that question is found on your website. One of the key strategies is to pump all your content out on your social media platforms—whether that's Facebook, LinkedIn, Twitter, or any other site where you engage with the public. Since you've already built a following of eager fans, they're more likely to click on the content to read it.

Google keeps track of every time they click and read content you're publishing. Google rates relevant content by the number of clicks an article or website gets from a particular zip code and how much time a visitor spends there. Once enough people click on your content and Google takes notice, when other people who aren't existing members search for the answer to those same questions, they're going to come across your content, because it's going to be scored higher than someone who's not as local or relevant.

PLAN TO SUCCEED

How do I start building a social media following? The first obvious step is to build your credit union's social media page. Make sure it looks, feels, and is branded like your credit union. Second, start building content and sharing it. Create a plan to populate your feed so people have a reason to like your page; the reason should be because you're offering pertinent and relevant information. In order to grow followership, plan for various content forms: informative content, an exciting and fun event, a creative contest, beneficial promotions, thoughtful and entertaining pictures, and so on. You don't necessarily want to promote the credit union with every post; you want to focus on promoting the community.

If you're a select employment group (SEG)-based credit union, you'll want to find out who the influencers of that select employer group are. If my SEGs are Giant Food and Walmart, then I probably want to make sure I like those pages and any other Giant Food and Walmart influencers. If you go around and like all those pages, you're getting social credibility into the social media space, and their influencers will begin to share things that become relevant to your community, because they're already part of that community. The same can be said for community-based credit unions. You will want to *like* the mayor's page, the pages of city council members, the key community organizations, the parks and rec department, town events, the library—anything associated with the community. The people who are going to value community are already paying attention to those other community organizations.

After you've built your page and liked the appropriate people and pages, start publishing valuable content. Start planning events, contests, promotions, pictures, fundraising, videos, and whatever else you think is relevant. Focus on providing educational content about key decisions and information that a member might need within your environment. Social media is about being timely, relevant, and engaging.

I highly recommend planning events. Not only are they a way to populate your feed with some content regarding the event itself, they're also an opportunity for your credit union to interact with the public face-to-face. It can be as simple as participating in something the community is already hosting, like a Fourth of July parade. Secure a booth or a float and start informing and engaging your following about your participation in the parade—don't forget to invite your followers to join you.

"We're going to be at the Fourth of July parade this Saturday, so come by and say hello! We're hosting a contest and the winner receives a $50 gift certificate to The Cheesecake Factory."

Public exposure like this invites your members to engage. Members usually bring their family and friends to events, too, so it's an opportunity to establish new contacts and potential new members.

You can offer promotions via your social channels, but I would tread lightly with them. You could say, "Anybody who's part of the social media group gets one point off their mortgage loan," or offer $500 off clothing costs, or invite members to participate in a "skip a car payment" program over the holidays. You can do all types of promotions, but remember: it's more important to find balance. The value is the community, not the promotion.

Other content ideas include offering a glimpse into the credit union, its staff and employees, or even the building. Social media was created for us to be social, and you can't be social without humans. Whether it's recognizing key employees or key members, make sure you're using this as a way to share relevant experiences and things that would make people want to be part of the community. Perhaps you're going through a renovation, or the building your credit union is housed in has fun, historical facts. All these things can be shared via social media. Take photos during the Fourth of July parade of your people working there. You should also include community members in those pictures, and publish them on your community feeds, asking followers to tag themselves or people they know.

Fundraising also produces content to share and opportunities to show you're connected to your community. Perhaps a credit union is a big supporter of a local nonprofit. That could easily produce several posts about the level of support, the nonprofit itself, and a call to action for others to learn about it. If something tragic happens in the community, credit unions have opportunities to host a fund drive or a special event to assist the family or group that experienced the tragedy. Social media is a great way to involve the community and show that you as a credit union really care.

SOCIAL MEDIA 101:

1. Go create a Facebook page, upload the CU's logo, and invite the management team and board.

2. Pick the top dog at each SEG and invite them; then create a special secret group for your secret shoppers and ask them a question or post an interesting article from the community every week.

3. Run a special promotion on the Facebook page and share some photos.

You should be able to do all of this in one to two hours. After the initial set-up, invest one hour per week moving forward to constantly engage your members.

Visit www.cu-2.com/facebook for a free Facebook 101 guide for credit unions.

CASE STUDY: PROVIDENCE CREDIT UNION

Brett Wooden, Chief Retail Officer of Providence Credit Union, has leveraged social media to engage his members. The effort began in 2016. Wooden wanted to prove that social media was valuable to his CEO and board, so he implemented strategies using a company called ChatterYak (CUSO). ChatterYak encourages people to like a page on Facebook and enters them into a contest to win a prize. ChatterYak then allows the credit union to ask questions, and that interaction creates lead generation.

The board was only involved in establishing a social media policy, which was approved with no problems. In its first attempt, PCU saw immediate results, garnering more than one thousand likes within the first few days. Contest prizes used weren't expensive, but had a lot of value—items like Apple TV or Chrome Cast, for example. Initial upfront costs were $2,500 and monthly costs were minimal, depending on the number of campaigns scheduled. In its most successful loan campaign, the credit union sold $2 million in new loans.

When asked how important implementing this strategy was to the credit union, Wooden rated it as a seven on a scale of one to ten. He said it greatly helped increase visibility and community involvement.

Moving forward, the credit union wants to see if there is a formula that would equate a certain number of likes to a certain number of members.

YELP

Much like Facebook, your members are looking to validate their decisions and conclusions. Yelp is a tool many of us use to find restaurants, lodging, and other services. My wife, for example, won't book a restaurant, hotel, or spa without first checking Yelp or Travelocity to find out what others think. It is important to note that members will read the reviews—both good and bad—to gauge whether they are buying something that will work for them. In addition, Yelp is pretty good at recognizing fake reviews, so you can't fabricate experiences and write about them. While Yelp is currently influential in restaurants, it isn't stopping there. According to a *Harvard Business Review* study, each star on a Yelp review equates to between 5 percent and 9 percent more business. Imagine if Yelp reviews had the same effect with local bank branches!

The key to Yelp starts with owning your Yelp account and setting one up for each branch. This can be cumbersome, but it is key for truly using it as a feedback tool, diversifying your feedback risk, and providing vital information to your members about a specific location. Since not all services are available at all locations, having independent location-specific information is key. It also allows you to upload different pictures and specifics, like whether or not a location has drive-thru or ATM services. When claiming ownership, there's a process by which Yelp verifies you're the owner, often using a phone number. This can be tricky for a credit union, since some locations have an "official" phone number unknown to the marketing department. Also, the phone verification doesn't play nice with automated phone systems. Yelp will then use an alternative method of validation, usually a postcard. This is also tricky, because they mail the postcard to the branch address. Even when a marketing department notifies the branch, these postcards have a way of getting lost or trashed.

Provided the marketing department has successfully navigated all the potholes and verified their "ownership" of the business, it can then respond to reviews. One credit union marketer shared his normal Yelp response:

Dear <insert complainers name>, at Random CU, we pride ourselves on exceptional member service. Clearly, we somehow missed the mark in this case.

I would appreciate the opportunity to learn more about your experience. If you have a few moments, I can be reached at xxx-xxx-xxxx, or email@email.com.

Thank you in advance for your time.

Sincerely,

Name

Head of Marketing or Service

He also shared that despite taking this approach, the complainer often never followed up with a call or email. Regardless, members and other Yelp users saw his post, showing that the institution cares, and that definitely matters. You can promote Yelp in your branches in an attempt to encourage happy members to write good reviews—your use of "*carpe* defect" (see Chapter 15) will surely help your chances of having members say great things!

If you've received some negative reviews, don't get too discouraged. Yelp's algorithm tends to suppress positive reviews in favor of negative reviews based on the tenure of users. If I didn't have firsthand experience being married to a Gen Y'er who regularly leaves crazy detailed and exact reviews, I wouldn't believe in their power. But in a world where everyone wants to be educated, make good decisions, and feel validated, Yelp is a critical path for your credit union.

YELP

1. Go create a Yelp account and claim your main office.

2. Review your existing member reviews (good and bad).

3. Respond to your negative reviews, and share your positive ones on Facebook.

4. Create a Yelp plan and process.

5. Please visit www.cu-2.com/yelp for our Yelp guide.

You should be able to do all of this in one to two hours. After the initial set-up, invest one hour per week moving forward to constantly engage your members.

10

SURVEY

Many credit unions validate their service with Net Promoter tools, and while I think Net Promoter is a good start, it's not a comprehensive tool. Yes, in theory, if a member is willing to refer you, that's a great indication of your services and the member's loyalty, but it neglects all the members who never get to that stage. Creating a repetitive process that allows you to continuously adjust and recreate good experiences for your employees is essential for receiving social validation.

Let me give you an example. I fly a lot, and every time I fly, I receive a survey from United asking how likely am I to refer the airline company to someone else. I might answer I'm likely to do so, because it was a good experience, but it doesn't address the real question of, "Do I ever refer airlines to someone else?" The reality is, I don't care how good my one individual flight experience was with United. On a collective level, the airline is so commoditized that it's a stupid question—and it certainly won't change my behavior. It doesn't encourage me to refer business, nor does it reflect my loyalty to the airline.

Credit unions have lots of repeated interactions—swiping a credit card, going to an ATM, calling a call center, etc. Since financial services are commoditized and fungible, it's not fair to measure loyalty on a transactional level; you have to look at it much more holistically. Loyalty comes from the way you make a member feel, among other intangible identifiers. Feelings come from experiences that are unexpected or highly differentiated. The brain is specifically designed to forget all the routine stuff.

Here is a quick test. Close your eyes and think about your childhood. After about a minute, what are the top three memories (good or bad) that immediately pop into your head? Most likely, they won't be routine stuff like brushing your teeth or mom making dinner. It might be dad making you dinner, though, because that might have occurred less regularly (no gender stereotypes intended). Either way, your brain is tuned to ignore basic day-to-day stuff over time and filter it out.

Tools like LiveSurvey are a great way to see a holistic picture. You're able to map the person at an intricate level when giving the service, the resolution to the problem on a one-on-one basis, etc. If something along the line isn't going well, you are privy to enough data to step in and fix it in near real time. LiveSurvey tracks each transaction and follows up with the member to solicit feedback. Every time a member calls the call center or walks into a branch, within a minute or two of that transaction, LiveSurvey is notified of the transaction within the system. It knows what, where, and who made the transaction and can immediately send a survey to ask valid experiential questions related to the transaction. Through the use of LiveSurvey, one credit union discovered its members were creeped out by how fast they were being greeted, how much everybody was smiling, and how focused the employees were on providing a really pleasant experience. Thanks to LiveSurvey's real-time feedback, that credit union was immediately able to tone down its level and perfect the experience for the member in a rapid-fire way.

If the airline surveyed me during the flight about how frequently the flight attendant was refilling my water, they'd receive feedback and immediately implement ways to fix any issues before the flight was over, which would have yielded a lot more loyalty from me than asking me for feedback after the flight had ended. If I complained because the flight attendant only gave me water once over a four-hour period and the airline now mandates an initiative for all flight attendants to give out more water, then that doesn't necessarily fix the complaint because other passengers might not want water that often. The survey is another great place to deliver educational content on Google keywords and traffic that matches your credit union.

SURVEY

1. Use Survey Monkey and create a three to five question survey about branch service. Pick one specific service—for instance, depositing a check.

2. Once a day, have IT run a report on in-branch check deposits.

3. Have marketing send an email with the survey to those members who performed the transaction.

4. Review the data once a week and make changes.

5. Please visit www.cu-2.com/livesurvey for free surveys to use with your members.

You should be able to do all this in one to two hours.

CASE STUDY: MAPS CREDIT UNION

Chris Giles, President of CU Wireless, weighed in on how MAPS Credit Union leveraged LiveSurvey from CU Wireless. In responding to negative Raddon member surveys, the credit union didn't want to wait two years to see if its strategies were working or not. MAPS therefore implemented weekly surveys, where it sent 200 surveys a week to relevant members. Although no board approval was necessary, Giles said he did inform the board of increasing the amount of surveys sent throughout the year.

An immediate glaring error in the beginning was setting up the results to be sent to one person. MAPS quickly modified that to be available to everyone in the credit union. MAPS then moved away from using Net Promoter and instead experimented with customer effort, which is a much better indicator of connection than satisfaction.

The strategy created almost an immediate shift in culture. Employees became more aware of their interactions with a member and the impact of those interactions on their personal and branch score for the day. The original intent behind the survey was to establish a continuous feedback loop after receiving results from a large survey MAPS conducted every two years through Raddon. Using LiveSurvey, the credit union was able to target feedback specifically to address issues identified in the larger survey. The true impact of these frequent surveys will be seen when MAPS receives results from its next big survey. Giles hopes to answer the question, "Did we improve in the key areas highlighted in the last survey?"

In conducting these weekly surveys, the credit union also uncovered some blind spots in its service delivery and has embarked upon efforts to address them. For example, MAPS identified process and communication gaps in its drive-thru's. These problems were uncovered through fairly consistent member comments and ran across branches. As the credit union implements strategies to remedy those problems, it's seeing a decline in negative comments.

LiveSurvey has also allowed MAPS to identify consistently high-performing branches and those with room for improvement. Plotting performance over time, the credit union can capitalize on best practices across branches and target improvement efforts at underperforming branches. In effect, the survey directs its attention to the areas where it can do the most good.

MAPS has been remodeling branches with a stylish, contemporary design. The survey also identified points of member confusion in the design, which allowed it to tweak subsequent remodels while remediating branches where the confusion existed.

Using LiveSurvey for episodic feedback has been quite helpful as well. For example, MAPS recently completed a conversion from Visa to MasterCard. Launching in two phases, it started with the credit cards and then used LiveSurvey to gather feedback from members in the process. MAPS asked about communications, the process, and opinions on the new product. This feedback informed its communication decisions for the launch of MC Debit, which was a considerably bigger project, impacting 70 percent of its membership. Afterward, the credit union conducted a follow-up survey. The results clearly showed that it was on target with member communications, and the launch was a success.

In addition to member surveys, MAPS also uses LiveSurvey data for employee reviews. They're the main focus of one-on-ones with employees.

Giles said that although results are difficult to quantify, members who have complaints are pleasantly surprised when the credit union immediately follows up. As for truly quantifiable, measurable results, MAPS still has training wheels on. Moving forward, MAPS wants to move even further toward a Customer Effort Score model instead of an NPS model, because the current five-question Likert scale doesn't feel like it's giving the credit union appropriate targets.

As a marketer and member-experience guy, Giles said he finds the most value in comments because members seem much more detailed in their feedback compared to the old days of paper-based surveys.

"You can easily sniff out changes in sentiment and performance based on comments," Giles said. "The LiveSurvey team is working on a sentiment-scoring model, which will be amazing. I'll be an early adopter of that process."

Before starting the process, Giles said he wishes he would have known about alternative survey methods since it would have avoided some "tough learning." MAPS spent about $12K a year, which was considerably less than a Raddon survey, which costs around $50K. Giles said using LiveSurvey was important and worth it because it brought the focus to member service, and that the conversation about member services has been greatly enhanced.

"From my perspective, the important thing is to start," said Giles, when asked what he would share with other credit unions. "Pardon all these clichés, but credit unions are great at paralysis by analysis, and letting perfect become the enemy of good. They want the perfect sample, the perfect survey, and the perfect answer. It's definitely a journey. As we continue engaging our members in continuous feedback, we're constantly learning—learning about the organization, member needs, survey techniques, and, often, how much we have yet to learn."

Visit www.cu-2.com/surveys for a free LiveSurvey tool for your credit union to use!

"HUG YOUR HATERS"

Oftentimes, credit union officials are reticent to engage with their most vocal and angriest members. If the person seems crazy as they rant away about his or her experience, we disconnect from the process and don't implement ways to try to win this person over.

That's the wrong way to react to the situation.

At the same time, credit unions readily endorse and have jumped on the Net Promoter system. That system is certainly better than traditional, once-a-year surveys, but it is fundamentally flawed, in my opinion. In most Net Promoter deployments, CUs take surveys after basic functions that are really table stakes. If you survey a member after completing an ATM transaction on their propensity to refer, it is a problem. As a consumer/member, I expect a certain set of things to work correctly every time. Those routine things don't create loyalty; they are just expected. However, it is the exceptional, unexpected, and over-the-top things that lead to raving fans and loyal members. When you consider that, looking at Jay Baer's methodology adds a lot more credence.

Jay Baer, an American marketing consultant and speaker, wrote a book called *Hug Your Haters* where he hits the nail on the head explaining that our haters aren't the problem: ignoring them is. His book focuses broadly on customer service across all industries and how all of them can embrace feedback to better their business—something credit unions need to do, too.

The first step is to identify the methods by which members can complain. They can mail a letter, yell at a teller, complain on social media, call a board member, or tell their friends. These are a few obvious ways people vent their frustrations. Understanding how your members like to complain will help you identify opportunities in how to engage with them and fix problems.

Just like planning the user experience for the first 100 days, you can hack the bad experiences that members have and turn them into good ones. In order to accomplish this, use Clay Hebert and Joey Coleman's Carpe Defect™ process (see Chapter 15). Start by listing all the things that the credit union or its employees get wrong on a regular basis. Prioritize the most frequent and high-impact ones, and brainstorm three to five potential solutions for each. For example, if you charge the wrong fee, you can reverse it, send a sorry letter with a $5 Starbucks card, reverse and credit it back, or offer a $10 donation to a charity of their choice. When you make the mistake next time, let the member service rep offer one of those choices to the member. You will blow their minds and turn a painful experience into a remarkable one. That's how you create raving fans!

In addition, using tools like LiveSurvey from CU Wireless to inject real-time feedback into routine experiences will help your team create and improve service over time. Instead of ignoring, shunning, or avoiding those who are critical of your credit union, learn to understand and use them as a tool to improve your business. Why is this person complaining? Why are they upset? How can you fix the situation and make sure it doesn't happen again?

The use of focus groups can also be highly beneficial, especially if you invite some of your unengaged members to take part. Take these members, or your haters, sit them down, ask them questions, and find out what they would expect you to do differently in order to earn their business. Focus groups are a good way for credit unions to learn how to bring value to their membership base, but a lot of credit unions don't include them in their strategies.

The newest way in which consumers like to complain is through public forums, specifically social media platforms. These situations open up opportunities to engage immediately with the complainers to address and fix their issues. You can address them publicly to show that your credit union cares, and then you need to contact the member privately and say, "I'm really sorry this happened. I tried to address it online, but I can make this right. Can we talk more about this and make sure that we address this issue?"

EASY WAYS TO TRY IT

1. Keep track of members who complained during the last month.

2. Look at the list of complaints.

3. Take the most common one.

4. Send a Starbucks card ($5 each) to those making the most common complaint, with a personal note asking them to be a secret shopper.

5. Gauge the response.

PART 4

———

EDUCATE AND EXCITE

In this section, we cover the E in DREAM. Credit unions are already considered some of the most trustworthy organizations—certainly way more trustworthy than big banks. Most credit unions, however, fail to educate digitally as part of their service experience. Sure, we offer seminars and workshops, but we can create much better digital experiences that help our members make better decisions through educational content.

Through education, we build trust, and through trust, we are able to sell.

The main challenge is overcoming the fact that most member services are not exciting. Mind you, I am not talking about doing everything the member asks, either. I'm talking about finding ways to wow and surprise our members that create loyalty, trust, and that truly differentiate credit unions from banks.

12

CONTENT IS KING

Teachers are rated as the third-most trustworthy profession—and they aren't far from the top. When someone takes the time to teach us something—not to be confused with selling us something—it shows us they care, they are helpful, and they are knowledgeable. Once we learn things, we are able to move down a path or thought process on our own. Keeping that in mind, let's look at the education to sales formula:

Educate = Trust = Sales

No one is going to know your community, your members, and your members' problems better than your credit union. Unfortunately, big banks like Bank of America have the resources to write the best articles answering all financial questions and publishing them with cool infographics that will likely blow yours out of the water. How do small credit unions get the content they've worked so hard on to appear in Google's search engines?

The good news is that media sources and feeds are manipulated. Google tracks everything and has found most people search for specific answers at a local level. Since you'll know more about your market than the Bank of America, it's essential to write content with specific details about your community using key data that other big banks don't have. Because people are often seeking detailed information about their community, they will be more likely to click on your content because of that data. Not only that, but Google prefers to send search traffic using a local filter, selecting the content that is most relevant to each user. If you're not creating local content, locals will not find you.

How do you create such content? If your members have questions, answer them. It's as simple as that. Answer the top fifty questions your members ask on a regular basis, as if you're sitting in front of them and having a conversation. Ask your tellers and member services reps what questions they hear the most. Understand the questions members are asking and then thoughtfully answer them in a brief and engaging way. (You might have to retool your approach.) Be sure to always think of ways to localize content, too: when's the best time to buy a house in your town, for example? "Here are the top ten banks in Greenville, North Carolina." Once you are the source of information, you become a trusted provider and a valid option for members, even if you don't include yourself on the list.

In those local pieces, you can write the same piece of content for all segments of your community. You could, for instance, write an article titled, "What's the best way for Nabisco employees to join a credit union?" You can then take the same article and rewrite it, geared toward the best way for Joe's Plumbing Company employees to join a credit union. You can reuse that content over and over again, but make it hyper-targeted at an age group, a population, an experience, or a region—whatever it is, target it in a way that Bank of America and other big banks can't.

Adding a blog section to your website, where users can search for previously answered questions, can be a great asset. Be sure to have a responsive website design, track keywords and SEO, and use Google analytics to better understand those who visit your website and what you can do to improve user experience (more on this in Chapter 13).

Publishing appropriate and relevant content isn't enough. In order to extract real value out of your content, you need to track what people are clicking on. Where do they go after they leave my site? Did they like the content? Was it displayed in a useful and well-written, well-presented manner? Were my examples good? These are key data points in figuring out what questions your member has, when they make these decisions, and how to write the appropriate content.

It's only through analytics that you will see if the question is coming from Google. Are all the questions coming from Google? What were the questions? What keywords am I not using and that my competition is using? How do I figure out where those data points are coming from and who is resonating with that content? Because if you see 100 clicks on how to buy a car, and you look at the analytics on Google and they're all coming from seventy-five-year-olds who can't drive, there's a disconnect you need to figure out and fix.

THE BASIC ROADMAP

When you look at the basic roadmap for content, it starts with those top fifty most popular questions a member might ask. How do I apply for a mortgage? How do I apply for a checking account? Why do I need a checking account?

Is a checking account better than a savings account? Answer those questions to educate your members.

Once you've answered the common questions, you can look at the goals of the credit union and strategize a content plan to reach those goals. If your goal is growing the size of your membership, or increasing car loans, or increasing deposits, start creating content surrounding those topics, because that's where you'll find the best bang for your buck. If you're looking to grow your membership, for example, then your content should answer the following questions: How do I join a credit union? Why should I join a credit union? What are the benefits of joining a credit union? What are the negatives of joining a credit union? What are the minimum requirements for joining the credit union? And so on. You can create a multitude of content answering questions regarding a single topic.

Content can also be an avenue for the CEO to establish a relationship and build trust with members. Your average credit union should have 500 to 1,000 pieces of content that explain how to do business with the credit union. Every time a member reads content you publish online, it builds trust. When content is king, your credit union is too.

CONTENT 101

1. Ask your call centers to create a list of the fifty most common questions members ask.

2. Write articles answering each question and publish them on your website/blog. Answer each question like you are sitting across from them at a Starbucks enjoying a cup of coffee.

3. Add Google Analytics on your website and watch it for a few weeks to find out what members search for the most.

4. Pick the top three search items and post one article a week to your Facebook page. If your members like it or comment on it, respond immediately.

You should be able to do all of this in four to eight hours. Invest one hour per week from that point on, and you will be off to better engaging your members.

CASE STUDY: TROPICAL FEDERAL CREDIT UNION

Amy McGraw, VP Marketing, and Mindy Partridge, CIO/CTO, weighed in on how Tropical Federal Credit Union leveraged content marketing to build its brand and consumer relationships.

TCU wanted to use more technology in engaging its members digitally. Its website was four years old, which is ancient in the digital world. It needed to look at the whole digital blueprint and review not only internal technology but marketing, advertising, and digital marketing.

Marketing automation was also missing. The credit union had no connections between CRM or digital leads, and it also looked to fill that gap. As it surveyed its marketplace and members, TCU created four personas based on its membership to help guide strategies.

In order to solve its problems, TCU integrated HubSpot data and lead-scoring into its content strategy. It also used algorithms and activity to catch attrition and keep an eye on competitor products. Once systems started talking, then automation kicked in. Adding the "I want to talk to someone" on the website also created several web leads. The board, which was tech-savvy was only a part of the process in approving the digital blueprint, according to McGraw. Board members didn't drive the process, but they understood its importance quickly.

The credit union also hired a full-time content person with a production and writing background who wrote copy and created video content for the credit union's website and social media. Keeping in mind the time or year, product timing, and combining everything with its four personas, TCU created a content calendar. Each blog/video was written targeting each persona, which was extremely helpful. "You need to know whom you are writing to," said McGraw. "It is about guiding the member on their journey. Our website and HubSpot were used to guide the journey—it focused on building trust."

Every section on the website contained a unique web lead form to which responses are given within a day, and generally within an hour. Within three months of launching its new and improved website, TCU implemented 642 webforms: 292 support, 200 consumer loans, 49 home equities, 46 new accounts, 38 financial reviews, and 17 business loans. Afterward, TCU created workflows and more content to address topics that fell within each webform.

The previous website design was static and had no optimization or tracking, nor did it use UTM (Urchin tracking module) codes. TCU also had an online app that was confusing and not mobile-optimized. All its applications were therefore mobile-optimized. Partridge said her staff never looked at real data to make decisions. "We used to throw our ideas at a wall to see what stuck," she said. "Now the data gives us direction. Our four personas were essential. We kill it on Facebook with auto loans, for example, and we're constantly working on improving the website to be a living, fluid thing."

Moving forward, TCU plans on moving 70,000 emails to HubSpot to facilitate lead nurturing and distribution of content. It determined print materials and brochures were no longer effective, since they're mostly thrown away. TCU therefore moved all its brochures to digital format and put them in the frontline teller/member service rep screens, so they could be emailed directly to members who wanted them. The credit union plans to build workflows around those brochures and member experiences using data, and to use marketing automation to facilitate the experience.

TCU also wants to use a mouse-flow analytics tool, which is helpful in knowing where things are located on each page and identifying waste in terms of bot traffic, which constituted a significant amount of the traffic on the website. TCU also wants to refocus more dollars away from traditional brick-and-mortar into digital.

13

WEBSITES 2.0

Twenty years ago, credit union branches were the number one place to have brand impact and build loyalty among members. Today, as more and more transactions are done electronically, your number one place to have a brand impact and a relationship with your member is through your website—and, as an extension, your mobile site. Your credit union's website is the number one spot for education and brand building. It's the most important connection you have with your members, and it's where you should devote a huge portion of your time.

I operate under the assumption that most people want to be well-educated and informed about the decisions they are making—and they more often than not use Google to learn, research, and educate themselves. If Google can't find your credit union's website within a search engine request, or if it doesn't see your website as being relevant and local, or if you don't have a beautiful website that engages your members and encourages them to spend lots of time on it, then Google won't rank your website, and your credit union won't appear to members searching for answers.

There are two main allocations of resources: budget and labor. An average branch costs a couple of million dollars to build, but your average website, which is where 90 percent of the brand impact is occurring, costs less than $100,000. Most credit unions are not spending anywhere near enough money on their websites, let alone spending enough budget or resources on defining and growing that experience to be leading-edge. The most important tool for your credit union is to have a functional website, which means it has a responsive design, and is content-enabled and social-media leveraged.

RESPONSIVE DESIGN

One of the most prevalent problems I've seen among smaller credit unions is that their websites aren't mobile-responsive—meaning when a user pulls the website up on a mobile phone or a tablet, the website doesn't respond to the smaller device, making it harder and more annoying to navigate.

Responsive web design allows a site's layout to change to the screen size being used. A wide screen display can receive a site design with multiple columns of content, while a small screen can have that same content presented in a single column with text and links sized appropriately to be read and used on that smaller display.

ENABLED CONTENT AND SOCIAL MEDIA

Another prevalent problem I often see is that most credit unions don't embed their content throughout their website, and instead focus on handing out brochures to educate their members on the services they offer. Printed brochures are poor tools to use to educate your members. This practice is not only severely outdated, but does a poor job of addressing a member's specific needs.

What if, instead of giving out a brochure, you educated the member through the website and made sure after that member left the branch, to follow up with an email saying, "You were in our branch talking about an auto loan and I wanted to pass along these three articles on our website that address how to buy a car." You can digitally track and maintain that relationship with the member throughout the life cycle, as opposed to trying to do it through a brochure, which just ends up in the trash. Plus, you help teach Google:

1. You solve that problem
2. Members trust you to solve that problem
3. Which keywords you are targeting for search traffic
4. How to help create consistency in your answers
5. Engage members in a one-to-many format

Social media is an avenue on which you can share your content and drive traffic to your website (see Chapter 8). When you look at websites that aren't tied into social media, they're not reaching as many people. Credit unions have a great opportunity to change that dynamic, but it's not as simple as building a new website. Once you establish your content and a strong social media presence, you might want to rebuild your website with those things in mind. My advice is to start with a comprehensive communications audit. Look at all the tools, media, and methodologies you currently use to interact with your members, prioritize them for impact, importance, and digital relevance, and then embed them in your website, social media, blog, call center, and branch transaction flows.

EVOLUTION OF THE CU WEBSITE

There's been a steady evolution of credit union websites over the decades. They first emerged in the late 90s as a business card, offering only an address, phone number, and some basic information. They then evolved to incorporate more information about the organization and its products, rates, and services. Today, it's evolved to this ancillary department that sits outside of the organization. You have to figure out how everyone in the credit union—every employee, teller, member service rep, and loan officer—is leveraging the website to enhance the member's experience.

You have to canvas not only how members are using the website, but also how your employees are using it. You have to build it so your members can self-service, but you also have to build it so your employees can use it to drive service expectations on a day-to-day basis. This means your employees need to be able to give members answers to their frequently asked questions through the website. The website needs to build trust through education and showcase the credit union's brand and style to its membership.

CURRENT TOOLS AND TECHNIQUES

I do not recommend using a proprietary content management system (CMS). Leveraging an off-the-shelf CMS, like WordPress or Drupal, is much more beneficial. If your marketing agency is trying to create a custom CMS, you'll encounter problems with speed and mobility as the technology changes. The advantage with an off-the-shelf CMS is it automatically grows, expands, and changes over time with its community of web developers. WordPress, for example, is an open source project that is reasonably secure and is part of an ongoing community which is constantly improving as new website technology, plug-ins, and widgets are created and implemented. The name of the game is to be as nimble as possible. It's vital to work on a platform that can easily evolve and plug in social media, content, or whatever comes next in our constantly changing world. If you're using a proprietary platform, this becomes a lot more challenging and time-consuming.

In order to receive analytics, you must imbed your Google analytics code on every page so you can track traffic and learn about consumer patterns: what pages they're landing on, how long they're spending on the page, when they're leaving, understanding your key words, and so on.

It's at this point that a marketing automation tool, like HubSpot, Infusionsoft, or Onovative, can offer more insight into your website's strengths and weaknesses, allowing you to further optimize and compare how your site is doing compared to your competition (see Chapter 16 for more on this). Use this to drive e-mail blasts and other calls to action and to embed site functionality using HubSpot or Infusionsoft to drive user flow and experience. You're also going to want to have some basic SEO (search-engine optimization) functionality. Don't forget to integrate widgets that connect to social media so your users have easy ways to share your content. Be sure to share your website content on Facebook, LinkedIn, Twitter, and so on, to drive traffic to your site. Something to also keep an eye on as you move forward is the use of video. Look at video content management systems and how to tie YouTube into your website. Think outside the box and figure out ways to create valuable content through video.

BONUS MATERIAL

For more tools, visit www.cu-2.com. For a free checklist for your new website, please visit www.cu-2.com/website.

EASY WEBSITE AUDIT

Circle yes or no to the following list. Work on the items you circle no on.

- Proprietary CMS = Yes/No

- Responsive Design = Yes/No

- Social Media Integration = Yes/No

- Google Analytics Tracking = Yes/No

- Marketing Automation (HubSpot, Onovative, Infusionsoft) = Yes/No

- Written Content/Blog focused on education = Yes/No

- Video Content = Yes/No

- Online Banking Login embedded = Yes/No

- You are proud of it and think it looks great = Yes/No

CASE STUDY: QUORUM FEDERAL CREDIT UNION

Bruno Sementilli, CEO of Quorum Federal Credit Union, leveraged a new website, along with digital branch technology, to implement automation within his branches. QFCU wanted more unrestricted access at employer branch locations, but space was always a limitation. A small footprint would allow the credit union to get that presence. It started with a kiosk-basically a high functioning ATM—and 90 percent of its transactions went purely digital. Going digital, as opposed to standard bricks-and-mortar, and was less expensive, so a low-population location worked well for as few as five hundred members.

"There are two things most important to our credit union: servicing members remotely and changing the business model so that 100 percent of our business is online," Sementilli said. "We don't open accounts via phone or at a branch; branches are strictly for advertising and sales. We have a branch with one employee and no transactions."

Updating the website was also a huge focus, since an online presence was a key requirement in the absence of a geographic member center. The goal was to be as simple as possible in every situation.

In terms of branch automation and technology, QFCU went through three to four manufacturers before it reached a functional level. (Several of these went bankrupt.) While member acceptance was good, the technical hurdles were challenging.

In terms of member adoption, QFCU focused on maintaining personal relationships and building trust, not only with members, but also with employees. For the credit union to introduce its new concepts to its members, it needed to make sure its employees were comfortable and well educated enough to then help them. This was key. Members were resistant at first. Doors were removed from the branches so QFCU employees could say, "Hey! We aren't going to be here all the time, so you may want to know how to use it when someone isn't here."

QFCU saw immediate results from branch automation. Some employees adapted well to the changes and were promoted; others were let go. QFCU closed five branches, and the ones that were left were managed with one or two people, which became a gateway to establishing a full digital relationship.

QFCU saw a more than 50 percent penetration rate with multiple products and online/mobile banking usage. This is particularly impressive since most of its members are obtained through non-traditional, indirect-lending growth strategies that tend to yield single-service members. The website should be seen as a credit union's entire operations area—anything credit unions are doing for their members needs to be 100 percent available online through the website. Be sure to enable self-service as much as possible.

QFCU's board had to be coaxed along to get them comfortable with branch automation. In regards to the website, MFA (multi-factor authentication) was a key challenge and became a board issue. Throughout the transition to digital branch banking, tracking became an essential function. Tracking the difficulties in the transition was key; the board wanted to see penetration, comparison with traditional methods, and off-line vs. online transaction volumes before going all in on the new strategy.

Some members have moved on over the years as they've shifted employers, but, according to Sementilli, the ones who have lived through the transition have noticed the difference. "You have to accept that you will not serve all members, and you will have some attrition," he said.

Credit unions need to focus on what they're good at. "We don't do auto loans, which was difficult for us to overcome," Sementilli said. "We don't do some things because we can't offer a better deal or a better service [than our competitors]."

14

WHAT IS GOOD MEMBER SERVICE?

The traditional ways credit unions try to measure good service don't reach millennials or highly digital-based credit union member expectations. When these service surveys are conducted, we usually see results along the lines of, "The CU is great and the people there are super nice. They mess things up a lot, but because they're so nice and they're easy to get a hold of, I keep doing business with them." As credit unions look ahead, that's not good enough. While it might be good enough to land a strong Net Promoter score, I don't think most credit unions are able to measure how they're doing on a per-employee, service, product, or transactional basis. The Net Promoter score is indexed with a range from -100 to +100, which measures the willingness of a customer to recommend a company's product or services to others. It is used as a proxy for gauging the customer's overall satisfaction with the company's products and services, and the customer's loyalty to the brand.

Credit unions spend a lot of money getting a new member in the door but very little optimizing the process once they're there. I liken this to brands that do a phenomenal job marketing themselves, but then you end up with a sour taste in your mouth when you show up and discover the experience doesn't match the marketing at all. Every time you have that disconnect between company and consumer, it causes friction. That's when loyalty erodes and people leave. Forty percent of members in financial institutions close their accounts within the first 100 days—which is such a waste! Here we've gone and made this brand promise. We've said, "Our credit union's awesome. You're going to have a great experience." Yet four times out of ten, the member is saying, "What you told me and what I experienced didn't match." An easy way to begin this process is to spend time thinking about that new member experience, because if you get it right from the start, everything else tends to work well afterward.

Here's a great example from OGO. When customers sign a contract, they receive a call from the implementations department kicking off the project. The client then receives a thank you letter that says, "Thanks for becoming a client of OGO." OGO spends a lot of time communicating with our clients to make sure they understand the process, expectations, results, and anything in between. Once they finish the onboarding process, which takes about sixty days, we send the credit union a cake with a note: "You just finished this great big implementation project. While it wasn't a piece of cake, have a piece of cake on us." It's a small investment that costs $100, which is almost nothing considering the average contract brings in between $20,000 to $30,000 a month in revenue. Clients who complete the install process and receive the cake at the end love us forever. The effort of making the first 100 days memorable and pleasant puts us in a position to be more comfortable when asking for a favor later on in the relationship. Or, say we make a mistake. They're more forgiving and give us a chance to fix it. In contrast, if we don't spend the time during the first 100 days, we've found that customers walk out the door at the end of the contract.

Once a member walks into the credit union, what does the experience need to be in order for them to stay? Lots of credit unions have coffee stations, cookie platters, or candy bowls stocked at all times. One credit union caused a buzz when they started giving out dog biscuits, welcoming dogs into the branch. By changing one little thing in the experience, you can garner a lot more loyalty. Now imagine changing twenty or thirty things in your new member experience. Impress them enough to garner that loyalty, and you'll start seeing new members move their entire financial relationships over to your credit union.

A TYPICAL EXPERIENCE

A member shows up to open an account. The credit union member service representative asks for a bunch of information, including a driver's license, and the member fills out and signs a lot of forms. The employee congratulates the member on opening up a new account, gives him a bunch of marketing crap, and he leaves to go home. The new member might feel content with the experience because it's a pretty standard one. Often, the credit union sends a welcome kit to the new member's home five days later. Inside, the message says, "We're really glad you joined the credit union. Here's your new member welcome kit where you'll find your checks, locations of all our branches," and so on. Then silence. The CU never says another word.

In the typical experience, however, the credit union never asked about the member's expectations, his needs, or what he cares about. Without this information, the credit union is setting itself up for some problematic situations.

First, most people under thirty years old don't want checks. I didn't use checks until I had kids and the kid economy forced me to! Second, modern banking is way too complicated to try and educate people about it in one sitting. Third, all of us learn differently: some of us are visual; others are auditory. What if, instead, the credit union had three or five paths to onboarding a new member that interwove communications from all levels—mail, phone, text messages, emails, and in-person? What if, by asking for some data points and mapping out the options, you could create a differentiated experience that was tailored to specific members?

Instead, my typical experience as a new member continues. Three weeks after opening my account, I visit online banking for the first time. I set up my username and password, log in, and am ready to conduct my first transaction. I try to transfer some money electronically from another financial institution—say $10,000—but the system comes back and says, "Sorry, we only allow you to move $1,000 at a time."

Well, that's annoying.

I call the credit union and say, "Look, my rent is $3,000 a month, so the $1,000 limit on my ACH isn't going to work for me. I don't know how to pay my rent if I can't move the proper amount. I don't know how to use you as a credit union if I can't pay my rent." The credit union employee replies, "I'm sorry about that, sir. We can change that setting. The maximum we can go up to is $10,000. Does that work for you?" I say, "Yes, thank you." The credit union changes the setting, the money is transferred in, and all is well.

A few days later, I log in to pay my rent, but when I try to set up the first bill payment, the system says the maximum amount I can write a check for is $1,000. That doesn't work for me, either, so I call the credit union again and say, "Now I'm trying to pay my rent, and it won't let me put a bill payment item in over $1,000."

"Oh, I'm sorry. That's a setting. We can change that. We can set it for $5,000."

Fantastic, thanks, but I could have avoided all that if the credit union rep had asked the right questions when I first opened my account. These first two interactions with this credit union are particularly bad because both of them were 100 percent preventable. In the account-opening process, if the credit union employee had simply asked some open-ended questions, all that would have been avoided.

"Mr. Drake, it looks like you're going to be moving some business over to us. What does your normal cycle look like? Do you do a lot of electronic transfers? Are they high-dollar amounts? How do you deposit checks? How do you like to interact with your financial institution?" With the answers to these questions, the credit union could have used that information to configure various settings and create the right broad profile for me on day one, and my experience would have been much smoother.

There is so much more a credit union can do in those beginning stages to leave a better impression on new members. Begin asking some of those questions early on in the process. Again, it doesn't have to be anything big or fancy. Even saying, "We just opened this account and it's going to be forty-eight hours before you can use it, because we're going to make sure that this works correctly for you." If the account is then approved fifteen minutes later and the credit union calls me saying, "We happened to finish this a lot sooner. We thought you should know your account is ready," you've intentionally told me it would take longer, which lowered my expectations, but because you've now over-delivered, you've created a positive experience.

As another example, if, in our conversation, you found out that I like to hike and I just moved to the area, do thirty seconds of research and say, "I know you said you like to hike. We asked some of our employees around the office and they said so-and-so is their favorite trail." You've successfully engendered loyalty through differentiation, and it hasn't cost you anything other than being thoughtful by defining the process up front.

As you look at that first 100 days and you think about the member experience from their perspective—they just moved to a new area, they're trying to get their stuff in order, they're trying to set up a new account, etc.—anything you can do to help smooth their experience could have a positive impact. Don't be shy in asking questions, either. If someone new walks into your branch and opens up an account, ask them: why? The new member might answer, "I just moved to the area." Great. Note to self: give him a coupon for a free pizza in the first week. These might seem like small-talk conversations, but the more you understand your member, the more opportunities you can create for your credit union to reach out and make a connection that will inspire that member to stay with you longer.

THE FIRST 100 DAYS

Do credit unions know how many members close their accounts in the first 100 days? My guess is most don't, but they should. Credit unions should know how much they spend to bring a new member in the door. They know if they spend X dollars of marketing, Y number of people are going to open an account.

Let's crunch some numbers and use the statistical information of a credit union spending $200 on average to bring a new member in the door—40 percent of whom close their accounts within the first 100 days.

100 new members * $200 per member = $20,000

40 percent close within 100 days = $8,000 lost

Net gain = 60 new members for $20,000

Cost per member = $333

Loyalty of 60 members = Who knows?

Now let's say a credit union spent some extra time and money exhilarating their new members:

100 new members * $200 per member = $20,000

**New member experience with wow factors =
$2,000**

20 percent closing within 100 days = $4,000 lost

Net gain = 80 new members for $22,000

Cost per member = $275

Loyalty of 80 members = High

Most credit unions don't know what the churn is, but it's an excellent indicator of what a new member's experience is like. It's essential to know how many people told me I sucked by walking out after only 100 days, especially since those who walk out aren't filling out any surveys.

Think of ways to differentiate and enhance a new member's experience. What can you do to make the experience smoother, better, pleasant, or exciting? If a new member recently moved to town, how can you assist in their move? If they are switching because they don't like another bank, how can you make the transition as effortless for the new member as possible? It's often a pain in the ass to switch financial institutions, so anything you can do to make the switch painless and add a little something extra will leave the member pleasantly surprised.

If a credit union that works with OGO declares some sort of disaster—basically a super-stressful experience for the guy on the other end of the phone—we automatically send a Starbucks card with a thank you note, saying, "You've probably had a tough night. Have a cup of coffee on us." We drop it in the mail and it gets delivered the next morning. We want to take a typically unpleasant experience and turn it into a more positive experience, and since our client isn't expecting it, the wow factor shines. We do it because going above and beyond the array of services we offer as a company leaves a better and longer-lasting impression—and that usually equates to happier and more loyal customers.

BONUS MATERIAL

Please visit www.cu-2.com/100 for a free first 100 day experience process.

ACTION ITEMS

Here are five easy experience builders for your credit union:

1. Set your call center hold message to intentionally tell the member it will be three to five minutes longer to access an agent, and then answer quickly.

2. Once a quarter, refund an ATM fee for any member in good standing. (Make sure you tell them or they probably won't notice.)

3. For new member accounts, say it will take an extra day or two to receive their new cards/checks, etc., and then deliver them early.

4. When they get a new car loan—and a new car—send them a free car wash coupon after the first month.

5. When members change their addresses, send them a checklist for updating all their other accounts (phone, utility, credit cards, etc.).

CARPE DEFECT

———

It's fair to expect that not every interaction is going to always be perfect; things will go wrong at some point. It's during these times that you have the greatest opportunity to fix the problem and instill loyalty in your members. It all depends on how the situation is handled.

Instead of being reactive—waiting for a mistake to happen and then fixing it—credit unions should adopt what Joey Coleman calls "*carpe* defect." The idea is that credit unions dissect each interaction they offer with customers and figure out all the ways each interaction can go wrong. From there, the credit union should prepare a tool kit to empower its employees on what to do in each of those situations.

For example, say I charged a member a fee when I wasn't supposed to. If the member calls and says, "You just charged me this fee you weren't supposed to," and I simply refund the fee, that certainly meets minimum expectations, but it doesn't wow or delight the member. If, instead, the credit union had a policy that said, "Whenever we charge a member a fee that we were not supposed to, we are going to give them a $5 Starbucks card," or "We're going to send them a personal note apologizing for the error and also explaining what we're doing to change the process behind the scenes to make sure that doesn't happen again." It's important to think about more than one solution to each potentially disastrous scenario, so your members have a choice. Each member will have different expectations, and credit unions should go above and beyond those expectations because that's what will leave the biggest impact.

I personally hate it when I call with a problem and the person over the phone says, "I fixed your issue and credited you back some money." It's a nice gesture, and while I appreciate it, it doesn't address the root of the problem. For example, I stayed at a Marriott once and had a terrible experience. I usually have great experiences at Marriotts, so when I received the Net Promoter score survey, I honestly wrote, "I wouldn't recommend this location because it was lousy..." and proceeded to describe what went wrong. I later received an email from the hotel manager saying, "Thanks for the feedback. I've credited your account with 7,000 points for your troubles. Have a nice day." Well, that pissed me off! I didn't want the 7,000 points—that wasn't the point of me complaining. I wanted the manager to train his employees better so they don't give that experience to someone else.

I suppose I might be unique in that regard. Some people might be thrilled to receive 7,000 points. Others might say, "I would rather have a free night," or "I would rather receive a refund." We all have different expectations of how we would like the situation to be handled, because we have our own definitions of what we think is fair. Your employees will also have different expectations based on their own ideas of what fair is, and it's important for the credit union to establish policies so nothing is taken too far.

Going through the "*carpe* defect" process and mapping out where problems can arise, you need to give your employees options to employ with disgruntled members. Giving three to five ways employees can fix a problem not only gives your members a choice, but it empowers the employees. "I know we charged you this fee when we weren't supposed to, would you like a $5 Starbucks card? Or would you like me to follow up with you and tell you how we addressed the issue so it doesn't happen again?

Or can I donate some money to your favorite community cause? Or would you like me to refund the fee and receive a personal note from our CEO apologizing? Which of these things would make you the most happy?"

As you look at ways to implement policies when things go right and when things go wrong, keep the bigger picture in mind. If one of your members has four things go wrong within a short amount of time, and you offer her a $5 Starbucks card each time, your gift cards now cheapen the experience instead of enhancing it. It's important to make sure these interactions are not seen as mechanical but genuine, because otherwise both your members and employees can game it and it completely loses its purpose.

PART 5

———

AUTOMATE

In this section, we cover the A in DREAM: how to take the four prior sections and incorporate them in your delivery channels. Many credit unions have an e-commerce department, but most of their delivery channels are not e-commerce. There are better ways to see your transactions. E-commerce is a mindset. It is about using all your digital engagement tools throughout your delivery channels.

16

MARKETING AUTOMATION

———

This section of the book covers automation. This is perhaps the book's most digitally intensive section. A credit union must reuse all its differentiation, education, exhilaration, and validation across all its delivery channels and create the omni-channel experiences that members desire. There are some new key technologies credit unions need to use, along with some old ones. Automation will take the form of internal solutions, external solutions, self-service, transaction, and outbound tools and approaches. Let's start with marketing automation.

Once you've created all the content about your credit union and the services it offers (see Chapter 12), how do you use it not just for inbound marketing, but to drive business throughout the member life cycle? That's where marketing automation comes in.

Each day your member does a couple of things that give you key insights into their lives, life stages, choices, preferences, and so on. Maybe they pay a big credit card bill, maybe they changed their address, maybe they added a significant other on their account. Whatever it is, these actions offer subtle clues about what they might need and what their experience has been with the credit union. Using data to determine all these subtle insights is great, but it isn't actionable yet. Marketing automation takes these insights day-in and day-out and turns them into actionable insights that allow you to create raving fans and grow your credit union.

Marketing automation refers to existing software that helps automate actions relating to marketing. Many marketing departments have to automate repetitive tasks, such as emails, social media, and website actions. Marketing automation technology makes these tasks easier. It ties all the different delivery channels, member experiences, and customer touch points together in well-defined processes that allow you to move the member from stage A to stage B, stage B to stage C, and so on.

Most credit unions communicate in the following ways:

- Statement messages and stuffers
- Direct mail
- Email
- Social media
- Website changes
- Call Center messages
- Branch signage

Your members are constantly seeing tons of messages, but most of these are big campaigns and sales pitches. To be highly impactful, you need to create tons of small messages aimed at self-service markets and experiences, so members can move through the journey on their time, at the right time. This requires content, data analytics, marketing automation, and other omni-channel coordination tools.

Marketing automation makes it easy for the credit union to communicate options and opportunities throughout these various life cycle stages—whether that's becoming a parent, retiring, buying a first home, or applying for a first car loan. Pushing that content through each member experience has a few notable advantages. First, it decreases the amount of time spent on the phone, and second, it streamlines answers so they are consistent across the board to all members going through the same life stage. Marketing automation eliminates a lot of noise and lets content do the work during these stage-by-stage, step-by-step interactions with members.

Once you've perfected the content within those stages, you can do A/B testing. You can inject additional marketing messages and influence into the equation to see different outcomes, and you can measure the results during each stage to figure out if one set of instructions is more useful than another, or if one piece of content is more useful for one demographic than another.

It starts with the front end. Most, if not all, credit unions are after growth—growing members, growing accounts, growing services, and growing wallet share. A lot of the first round of big-impact items, and the easiest one to model, starts with the new member experience, especially because if you nail the new member experience, members are more likely to forgive future errors or mess-ups in the rest of that life cycle and become loyal to the credit union.

The starting place is your website landing pages. You want the site to answer any and all inbound questions people are typing into Google. You'll need something like HubSpot, Onovative, or Infusionsoft. (There are a fair number of marketing automation tools in the credit union space to choose from. I've had good experiences with HubSpot and Onovative.). Most don't do anything web-related, however.

They send email blasts, text messages, and direct mail, but seem to neglect the number one place members go to first—the website. I think credit unions need to start with pull—as opposed to push—automation, because that's where a lot of new opportunities exist. A solid, informative website is your biggest opportunity to grow, retain, and build relationships straight out of the gate.

Most credit unions have landing pages that say, "Here's our auto loan rate, and here's how to apply for an auto loan," but they can't correlate that to the member who actually landed on the page. Credit unions don't have the analytics or tool kit that allow them to correlate the members on the site and what they're interested in, or to relay information or content to other people in the organization. By using HubSpot, for example, a credit union would see the analytics around what a member's natural curiosity is and the research they're doing before they take action. That early-stage information becomes extremely helpful in driving the member experience throughout the rest of the process.

Once you put the tools in place and have mapped the content and the keywords to understand why people are visiting your site, you can start using it on your website *and* within online banking. You can also embed your content into social media or as an email to the customer saying,

"We noticed you were on the website looking for more information about auto loans. Here's our guide to how to apply for an auto loan." You can then track members' online interactions. If they clicked the link you sent, you can better gauge their level of interest and need.

You can keep score of each member's actions, so when they hit a certain level and come into your branch, you can bring the topic back up again and say, "We noticed you were interested in this, is it something you're ready to move forward on?" You can now ask for their business, as opposed to selling the business.

FIRST THINGS TO TRY IN MARKETING AUTOMATION

1. Start by selecting something that is routine but doesn't require real-time data analytics: for example, the member opening process.
2. Map out the first 100 days, what should happen, where, and when. Create decision trees for when members naturally choose the best way to serve them. For example, use a content piece targeting cherry-pickers or rate shoppers versus one targeting loyalty. (This should give you great insight into how the member shops).
3. Insert some surprise and delight into the new member process.

4. Create five or six articles or educational pieces explaining what the first-time member will experience and send at least one communication in every medium: voice, video, text, email, and physical mail.

5. With your next 100 members who open accounts, have fifty go through the old process and fifty go through the new; track the results after 100 days.

BONUS MATERIAL

Please visit www.cu-2.com/automation for a special guide on how to use automation in your credit union.

17

MEMBER SERVICE AND SALES TOOLS (CRM)

The previous chapters were dedicated to how to build a different service experience: you've implemented marketing automation; you've looked at and analyzed your "*carpe defect;*" you've empowered your employees with options to handle member complaints; and you're using Live-Survey to fix your goofs in real time. Your online content is educating members and potential customers who are receiving validation through social media, and now you need to do the essential task of asking for their business.

Unfortunately, credit unions tend to look at "sales" as a dirty word. Most credit union officials say, "I'm uncomfortable asking my member for more business." The problem comes down to when people think of sales, they tend to think of a used car salesman. They don't tend to think of salespeople as educators or trusted sources of information. We also live in a "buyer beware" culture, which makes it more challenging to sell the useful services credit unions offer. In the past, the only way potential consumers learned about a credit union's services was by personally asking credit union employees face-to-face. That doesn't happen anymore, thanks to the Internet and massive search engines like Google. Nowadays, when someone is thinking about applying for a car loan or opening up a retirement account, the first thing he or she does is go online.

If I stumble across your credit union's content and it answers my questions, your website—and therefore, credit union—brought value to me personally. That value inherently builds trust, since the credit union is demonstrating its competency, and I'm more likely to do business with it. If I walked into that branch, it would be a good opportunity to sell me on one of the credit union's services I've clearly shown an interest in, since I visited one of your pages. Credit unions need to stop viewing sales with a used car mentality and emphasize an educational mentality. Our job is to educate and build trust with consumers and then ask for their business at the right time.

In order to do that effectively, you need a CRM (customer relationship management) system, so you know which life stage members are currently going through, what information they've looked at online, and how they've been educated, so you can support them along the way. Say a member is on your website looking for an auto loan. She's clicked links to four or five different articles about it, figured out where she wants to buy the car, and even filled out the forms. These actions should trigger the CRM to ask for her business. The CRM alerts a member service rep to capitalize on the opportunity, since the member is well educated and knows what she wants. A service rep should call and say, "I've noticed you're thinking about buying a car. What can I do to help you?" This is a much better approach than trying to convince a member who already owns a car that she should get an auto loan.

Why do credit unions struggle so much with sales and service? Over the past twenty years, I have watched the industry and credit unions I worked for struggle with being sales-driven. The reality is that sales is part of the industry. Educate and train your staff to view sales as a positive and necessary part of the business, that it's a way to teach and help members by recommending products and services. Better yet, hire people who are naturally helpful and like to teach. One of my favorite interview questions is, "Tell me about a time you helped someone that you didn't have to?" You'd be amazed at how many people can't give you an answer—which tells me they're probably not great at service!

Once your team realizes asking for business isn't dirty, you'll be surprised at how quickly business increases. You must make the change, though. The challenge is dealing with employees who are uncomfortable with asking and selling. New and emerging technology won't solve this discomfort. Creating a well-designed CRM for employees who won't go after closing sales is of no use. In my experience, you have to figure out which staff members want to use data to drive their interactions with members, and give them sales roles. Pay attention to those who like to teach, as they tend to fit the role well. Anyone who doesn't fit needs to be moved into a different role or simply let go.

To create a sales and service environment, you need the following:

- The right people
- Educational content
- A CRM
- The right reinforcing processes
- Grit

Imagine you ran a hospital and required data from your nurses every step of the way. You wouldn't let some people do it and not others. The CRM and a sales process are the same. Everyone must be part of the system. It isn't hard to do, but it is a different way to work. Look at ten or fifteen business processes that you could improve if you had the proper data, then make sure they require people to start entering data. These could be marketing, HR, accounting processes, or any number of things. Teaching your employees to teach is much easier than teaching them to sell. If they educate, they'll earn members' trust, and once trust exists, they just need to ask for the business!

EASY WAYS TO TRY IT

1. Watch your MSRs or call center reps.

2. Categorize them into educators vs. transactors.

3. Give the educators some additional tools, like blogs or content, to refer members to.

4. Have the transactors follow up in a week to ask the member to follow the credit union on Facebook. Measure how many actually do it versus how many avoid the work.

5. Have the educators follow up in a week to make sure the question was answered and ask the member to follow the credit union on Facebook. Measure how many actually do this versus how many avoid the work.

CASE STUDY: FIRST TECHNOLOGY CREDIT UNION

Read the following case study about the cultural changes and the technology First Technology Credit Union implemented. CEO Greg Mitchell weighs in on how he has leveraged sales and service technology to facilitate growth across several years.

FTCU needed to figure out how to be relevant in the face of huge FinTech innovation and the growing irrelevance of traditional financial institutions. FinTechs were taking market share rapidly. The credit union needed to change its culture from one of entitlement to one of member advocacy. Its products and distribution were stale and it didn't know its members, who wanted FTCU to be their advocate.

The credit union therefore rolled out Salesforce and Terafirma. Salesforce is a digital sales platform and Terafirma helped create a consistent experience across all delivery channels. Salesforce tracks member activity across all channels and enables high visibility, which means a better member experience across the entire platform. FTCU's first implementation of Salesforce did not go as well as planned; the credit union promised too much and couldn't deliver. It then moved to an agile deployment strategy instead of a perfection strategy.

"Historically we were told our people couldn't do this, that our technology couldn't do this," Greg said. "We couldn't do it without negatively impacting the member experience. You have to make the tough calls and have the fortitude to muscle through the difficult parts to make the cultural changes."

After muscling through those difficult bumps in the road, FTCU saw resolution in the call center rise from 42 percent to 82 percent within the first year and realized an immediate reduction of $4 million per year in fraud losses. The credit union also saw a 15 percent year-over-year growth, achieved $9.5 billion in assets, and had a 1.23 ROA. It was able to remove the vast variability that occurred across its delivery channels and products, and offer super consistent member experiences regardless of where the member starts and finishes the process. Members said there was tremendous value added, since it allowed members to transact with the credit union in much simpler and more efficient ways.

Although no vote was necessary, FTCU filled the board in early during the process and made meaningful investments in tools and approaches.

"We have a sophisticated board," Greg said, "which understood the importance quickly."

Greg said the CEO sets the tone and the culture. Once he decided what business the credit union was in, he then moved to find a solution and had the courage to make it happen no matter what the cost. The question he kept coming back to was, "Do we want to be relevant?"

Moving forward, FTCU is actively working to partner with FinTech startups—who don't have eyeballs but have imagination—to leverage their innovation. "We have found this to be a huge opportunity to be relevant with our members and to leverage outside innovation in a win-win scenario," Greg said.

When asked what he would share with other credit unions, Greg said, "You need to be a leader, make the tough decisions, and do what is right for the member and the organization above what is right for you."

18

ONLINE BANKING

Online banking evolved from paper statements because someone thought, "Boy, it would be a lot better if we had electronic statements," eliminating printing and delivery costs and providing members with their statements much more quickly. I remember early online banking, before Internet banking, when my father would take a phone coupler modem and hook his laptop up to it, dial in to Bank of America, download all his transactions, print them out locally and then balance the checkbook, instead of waiting for his statement to arrive in the mail. Then the Internet came and made the process easier, eradicating the phone coupler, the slower modem, and the need to balance the checkbook. Online banking, however, was still pretty basic.

Eventually you had the addition of bill pay, which—in my opinion—is what made online banking stick, because it added a lot more functionality and usability for your average member.

Advances in banking through the Internet continue, and we see online banking providers evolving into personal financial management (PFM) and online mobile wallets, along with much more. Companies like BankJoy or Narmi Technology are popping up, offering a single platform for banks and credit unions to drive functionality across all the different delivery channels—not just online banking. One of the major challenges I see among credit unions is their singular focus on online banking, while ignoring mobile banking, wallets, mobile workforce, and their intersection with the website. Online banking in the next generation needs to be ubiquitous across all these different platforms and designed with a containerized approach, so you can reuse the same functionality, not just online, but also on phones, tablets, wearables, and so on.

Many providers are offering much more robust ecosystems and containerized approaches, allowing you to use that functionality over and over again in different use spaces, mediums, and devices. This next generation of tools needs to be designed with that same responsive design and functional toolkit, with the website tying everything together. In addition, systems need to leverage data, use social media, and most importantly, educate throughout the platform.

Once you have all of those delivery channels and platforms working together, you can drive interaction and deliver value to members on their time, wherever they're at, and how they want it, successfully conveying the convenience they expect. Today, I can visit Amazon on a desktop, on my phone through a web browser, through an app on my phone or tablet, or through a device like Amazon Echo. As a consumer, I expect to have a certain set of functionality across all my various options. It's also important to note—whether it is Amazon or Facebook—most entities these days provide multiple apps for functionality. They don't try to jam all into one, which would be clunky and unusable.

What's also important to keep in mind is that all of this will change, and we need to keep up with such changes. Something new will be created down the road, and the quicker the credit union adopts new technology or platforms, the better position they'll be in. Every day you wait is another day you're behind.

These constant changes and improvements to our technology will one day render the way we now bank online obsolete. As technology moves more toward mobile, wearables, and voice recognition, we won't use a browser to access our credit union anymore. As we continue toward a future rich with functionality, it's far more likely that we'll verbally dictate commands to our phone, watch, or other device yet to be invented. "What's the balance in my savings account at Sunshine Credit Union?" The device will respond with the balance, and you can then command it to send money. "Great, send $53 to Mom."

As humans, we're accustomed to verbalizing instructions or directions and receiving an intelligent response—as if we're talking to another human. The idea that we'll continue interacting with our mobile phones or through applications is wrong. It's vital for credit unions to pay attention to these technological advances and keep an eye out on how to capitalize on and use them to continue improving our membership experience. The irony is that it will probably come full circle to interacting with an analog of a person who follows artificial intelligence playbooks— think Data from Star Trek.

NEXT GENERATION ONLINE BANKING REQUIREMENTS

At the bare minimum, you should have the following. Circle yes or no; work on those you don't currently offer.

- Integrated into website = Yes/No

- Members self-select username = Yes/No

- Members self-select and can reset password = Yes/No

- MFA (multi-factor authentication) solution is usable = Yes/No

- Integrated content options = Yes/No

- User can see whole financial picture (credit cards and mortgages usually are stand-alone) = Yes/No

- User interface is modern and simple = Yes/No

- Works in all browsers = Yes/No

- Works with MINT or other PFM (personal financial management) software = Yes/No

- Credit union can do promotions = Yes/No

- Collects and gives data to the credit union = Yes/No

- Enables delivery of embedded educational content = Yes/No

- Builds trust with the member = Yes/No

- Validates member decisions = Yes/No

- Solves member problems = Yes/No

19

MOBILE BANKING AND WALLETS

Everybody knows mobile is a key component to success in our digital world, since businesses in every industry need mobile apps. There's a huge opportunity for credit unions to own their brands and member experience, and deliver value in a way they haven't historically. Similar to the evolution of checking your statement online on a weekly basis, as opposed to waiting for a printed one once a month, mobile wallets will allow you to check your bank statements and the status of your accounts multiple times a day, whenever you want. You could check it with every transaction, if you wanted to.

In this ever-present, daily interaction ecosystem, the ways credit unions can insert themselves into the member's life presents a unique opportunity to add a ton more value—whether it's through facilitating a payment, providing better rewards programs, helping members book a table at a restaurant, or extracting cash out of an ATM. We need to move from single-dimensional products, like an ATM or debit card, into multidimensional products, because smart phones add data and context to every transaction in ways single-dimensional products can't.

In addition, because the cost of deployment is so much less per member in the mobile environment than the traditional single product, you're going to see an explosion of innovations and ideas.

Looking forward, it'll be hard to make the argument that online banking will be more relevant than a digital wallet, given that the wallet is much faster and more consistent. And it's not like there will be members sitting on their phones using their digital wallets for long periods of time, either. They'll be using it for a minute or two while they wait in line here and a minute while they wait in line there, so the efficiency of delivering that information and understanding how they're using it will be key.

A MOBILE ROADMAP

There are two ways credit unions can look at a mobile roadmap. Does it start with mobile banking and expand to wallet, or does it start with wallet and gives way to mobile?

You can say, "Online banking gives way to mobile, mobile gives way to wallet, wallet needs to have some functionality in it" and go from there. Or you can say, "We're going to skip three steps and start with wallet. The wallet will have a database of merchants, it'll show my ads and offers, and it'll also be useful without such real-time information. It'll have the rewards program, it'll enable users to make basic payments, and eventually we'll embed mobile functionality in it." Historically, the bill pay feature was what triggered this in online banking. With digital wallets, the focus will be on the transaction, research information, and the member's ability to land a better deal. Through those features, value comes from the monetization of data on where people are spending money, when they're spending it, and how they're spending it. It's no longer about signing in to check an account balance.

Wallets simplify steps and offer users more convenient ways to conduct transactions. If you get on eBay, for example, and want to list a product, you have to pull up the website, take pictures, somehow get those pictures onto your computer, upload them, fill out the listing details, put in a dollar amount, and then finalize the listing and publish it on the website. If you use the mobile app, however, all those technologies are blended together on your phone. You can use the phone to take pictures and the app automatically uploads them into eBay. You can add your information, fill out the questions, click okay, and instead of taking ten minutes to list an item, it takes three. Mobile wallets follow the same trajectory.

Bill pay is already evolving into this mode. One company, Allied Payment, uses a technology called Picture Pay. Would you rather sign into bill pay via online banking and enter all the necessary information, or would you rather use your phone to take a picture of your bill and simply click the pay button? Consumers will opt into whatever is easiest and most convenient. Forget the work, effort, and history of old bill pay methods. Move to the new way and enable your members to use your services more easily. Review the usage of your "A" members from analytics and give them different payment authorizations than your less loyal members.

In addition, we are seeing an evolution of many different payment tools—Apple Pay, Samsung Pay, LevelUp, MasterPass, Visa Checkout, and so on. Members will have ten or twenty different financial institutions, and their wallets will be able to mash them all together in a way that's easy and convenient. You want your phone to be able to pay for things every time you go out, instead of just 70 percent of the time.

Other new features on the horizon include cardless cash access, order ahead from LevelUp, pay-as-you-go car loans, instant loans, peer-to-peer payments, and loyalty and rewards programs. In five to ten years, we won't have a driver's license the way we do today. It'll eventually be embedded digitally on our mobile phones or wearables. Eventually, people won't want to carry their AmEx, Visa, Best Buy, and credit union cards, either; they're going to want them in one easy-to-use device that they already take with them everywhere.

QUICK MOBILE FEATURE LIST

Circle yes or no to the following items; work on those you circled "no." Disclaimer: Mobile banking is changing rapidly. Please visit www.cu-2. com for an updated list.

- Check balances and transactions = Yes/No

- Deposit checks = Yes/No

- Picture pay = Yes/No

- Peer-to-peer (via email or mobile number) = Yes/No

- Schedule appointments with the CU = Yes/No

- Chat with the CU = Yes/No

- Report lost or stolen items = Yes/No

- Receive alerts = Yes/No

- Branch or ATM locator = Yes/No

- Cardless cash access = Yes/No

- Order ahead = Yes/No

- Rewards = Yes/No

- Adds and offers = Yes/No

- MFA for your online banking = Yes/No

- Mobile wallet = Yes/No

- Collects and gives data to the credit union = Yes/No

- Enables delivery of embedded educational content = Yes/No

- Builds trust with the member = Yes/No

- Validates member decisions = Yes/No

- Solves member problems = Yes/No

CASE STUDY: DIGITAL CREDIT UNION

Watching the evolution of mobile payment technology was difficult for David Araujo, VP IT at Digital Credit Union. He wanted to observe how members transact business with mobile transactions and saw the need to stay current. He therefore looked at Apple Pay, Samsung Pay, Android Pay, and CU Wallet. Although it didn't use any specific tools, the credit union used monthly reporting on data and statistics on all these channels: watching Apple Pay, Samsung Pay, Android Pay, CU Wallet, etc., as well as getting transaction counts and dollar volumes. Some of the various approaches included person to person (P2P), balance transfers, CU Wallet deployment, and offering the ability to pay non-DCU loans. Money movement needed to be as easy as possible; mobile payments were simply an extension of this. The goal was to create an engaging digital mobile-payments solution that helped DCU stay ahead of its membership.

One strategy, P2P (peer-to-peer), didn't work at first, but DCU's fortitude eventually paid off. Despite not being overly successful with P2P initially—the adoption was challenging—the success rate improved after a few months. Although this functionality has existed for years, adoption began later and new functionality is being embraced much faster. This approach has been important to the credit union, because it is a technology leader and this is key in its strategy. Members have said there is tremendous value added because it allows them to transact in much simpler ways. Everything but merchants is driving huge value to members.

Ultimately, the credit union found that, as it gets members into the DCU digital world, they can constantly evolve and improve the experience by injecting new technology along the way. Each time, it seems like members adopt the new stuff faster. The key was to be the first to enroll and begin moving them down the path!

DCU uses the Carver board governance model. The DCU board receives monthly updates, which cover DCU's innovation and leading-edge initiatives and experiments, and results are shared with the board. No board approvals were necessary to advance the digital strategy. Introducing DCU Pay at the merchant level is next. DCU wants to go to market using LevelUp to enable ordering ahead on both the Android and iOS platforms.

When asked what he would share with other credit unions, Araujo said, "Try and keep current. Keep investing in different things."

20

BRANCH AND CONTACT CENTER TECHNOLOGY

On the surface, branch technology hasn't changed much. Sure, we have more things plugged in to our PCs and laser printers, but for about ten to fifteen years, the signature pads and PC environment have been pretty consistent. What we're beginning to see in branch technology is a digitization of the member experience. We're seeing functionality from websites, online banking, mobile, and other channels emerge within the branch, so tellers or MSRs interact with each member more holistically and less transactionally.

Most members nowadays research in order to feel informed enough to make good decisions for themselves and their loved ones. Gone are the days of members expecting MSRs to "sell" services to them. What they are seeking instead is a better overall experience with transactions that flow through their life stages in ways that are best suited for them. Unfortunately, credit unions are recreating a lot of functionality in branch technology instead of containerizing and reusing what already exists within online banking, an approach that of course costs them more.

Through systems like remote teller kiosks, iPads, and educational displays, credit unions are shifting to technologies that emphasize self-service and simultaneous interaction, allowing them to be more efficient and add more personalization to the member experience. Remote teller kiosks aren't meant to replace tellers completely: they allow members to complete simple transactions on their own with a service coach standing by, ready to jump in and engage, if necessary. Instead of just a transactional interface, a kiosk allows the credit union to dig deeper and build a more enriching experience. It also establishes a better relationship with members by having higher caliber employees who spend less time on simple transactions and more time on relationships. Basic work functions can be offloaded to self-service technology and more advanced conversations, like product selling, can be left to MSRs, which one credit union calls MEAs—member experience agents. This set-up changes the flow of the branch to be more modular and pod-based—similar to the Genius Bar at Apple, which is much more inviting and open, and much less claustrophobic than a traditional bank. Apple, a company outside the financial industry, has defined a new experience that financial institutions are replicating—probably the biggest impact on branch design of anything in more than twenty years.

Branch technology has two facets: how the technology affects the design and the physical appearance of the branch, and how it is used in the branch. It is important to note that the branch environment should be designed to differentiate and personalize based on data, educate, excite, validate, and automate. If the credit union fails to stay true to these principles, it will violate its digital brand promise and all this e-commerce work will be discounted in the member's eyes as a major failure, leading to an erosion of trust. Without trust, you can't help the member.

From a design perspective, credit unions should consider offering more of a community center than the lobby experience traditional banks typically offer. Consider creating an inviting lobby area with open workspaces, where members can work or conduct conference calls, connect to free wireless, and enjoy some coffee and snacks. With a new design layout, self-service kiosk placement means the credit union won't be required to maintain the same cash management policies and processes, either. If the credit union is designed with self-service kiosks, you can treat it more like a sophisticated ATM, which means MSRs have more time to focus on educating and building trust using digital tools.

There are options aplenty with multiple types of kiosks for the choosing. Some are built for simple transactions, while others can interact with a call center for more detailed ones. There are also kiosks that are more educational, working as amalgamations of the credit union's website to educate and build trust with the consumer, reusing containerized website content.

Ultimately, more and more routine transactions can be offloaded onto online banking, mobile banking, and call centers. Traditional branches have a different function today than they did in the past. Since most selling occurred organically in branches using soft sales skills, this change is causing a real shift for credit unions. The branch of the future is seen as a high-tech Genius Bar serving the community. However, I am not sure credit unions or banks have figured out how to turn their branches into community centers. If we use REI as an example, its brick-and-mortar experience incorporates rocks to climb with new shoes, tools like extra weight to try on back packs, and stands for trying out bikes. The company turned into an experience center and conveniently sells related items in its store. The primary job of the REI representative is to educate—not sell—and help consumers make the best decisions.

The local bank in my town partnered with a coffee shop and called itself "Pony Espresso"—an awesome name for a bank and coffee shop if you know Wells Fargo's history. The branch has MSR stations and an espresso bar. Credit unions can learn a lot from this arrangement. Perhaps they could have a financial tune-up station where you could review your accounts for cash-flow leaks. Or maybe the branch could be organized around key financial decisions like lease vs. buy or rent vs. own. Or, it could function as a small business startup center. The credit union could even have a digital security station where members could shred documents and learn strategies for how to protect themselves from fraud. Or, a car ownership station could offer free car vacuums, window wipes, or access to a car-seat installation expert. Each station could be designed around the most common problems members face, teaching them how to make good decisions.

Once enough content is created for the website, study your analytics and alter, reuse, and repurpose bank technology to enhance the digital experience in the branch, while simultaneously providing real-time validation or perspective from life stage experts (i.e., humans). Credit unions need to rethink the entire experience and focus around the idea that members are usually trying to solve a problem when they come in the branch or call the contact center—they want a car, not a car loan. I know if my credit union incorporated even one or two of these ideas, I would stop in or call more often—and in doing so, build a relationship and create the opportunity to make me feel like I owned the place and become more loyal, thereby garnering new business.

BRANCH ROADMAP

Your roadmap doesn't start with replacing all your teller lines. It has to be gradual, otherwise you'll surprise your members—and most people don't like abrupt changes. Credit unions can slowly implement new technologies that introduce the notion of self-service. As members grow more comfortable with doing transactions on their own with these remote kiosks, the credit union can begin to focus on other things. Do we need tablets in the branches that allow the member service representative to walk up and share information or book a loan? How do we deal with electronic documents? The roadmap starts by looking at each piece of the technology and what impact it will have. It's important to dissect the entire experience to avoid any pitfalls. For example, one credit union redesigned and remodeled its branch with a beautiful lobby and remote kiosks, but they forgot to incorporate privacy in its layout design—the kiosks were too close together. To fix the problem, since it was too late to redesign and physically move the kiosks, the credit union installed inexpensive IKEA bamboo screens to separate the kiosks sitting next to one another.

When it comes to technologies that enhance a user's experience, I encourage you to think outside the box. For example, why are we still relying on driver's licenses for proof of identity? Couldn't we move toward voice recognition, facial recognition, or fingerprint verification to make it easier—and safer—for members to identify themselves? If those tools were built into the branch's flow and design, they would certainly make for a much more holistic member experience that is not only unconventional and cool, but also convenient and safe.

Imagine the branch of the future, where you walk in and facial recognition software identifies you. It looks at your account and can trigger things you might be interested in, based on your exterior Facebook feed, so the member service representative in the branch can be notified what those services are. The MSR won't ask you for an identification card. He'd approach you to have a conversation about your needs, answer any questions, help facilitate the entire process, and ask for a quick signature on an iPad—and you're done. We can recreate the entire experience without the traditional barriers of a normal bank environment. We just need to be a little creative.

CASE STUDY: PIEDMONT ADVANTAGE CREDIT UNION

In 2014, Judy Tharpe, President and CEO of Piedmont Advantage Credit Union, started focusing on branch automation and technology to add intrinsic value to her membership, especially since it was aging and she wanted to change that. The credit union used Filene Research Institute's research on millennials and found that they are an extremely different generation. Credit unions have been built around baby boomers, so the approach to attract younger people needed to be updated. Just like most credit unions, PACU wanted to lend more money but couldn't because its average member age was 47 and the loan needs weren't as strong among that age group. In its quest to attract younger members, PACU tested simple concepts and experiences and discovered millennials, despite their high confidence in topics surrounding finances, didn't actually have any knowledge behind them. PACU therefore offered auto buying seminars, for example. It built solutions around these educational opportunities and made them about the experience, rather than only focusing on the product.

PACU's mission is to enhance the lives of its members, so naturally it wanted its employees and members to feel like they were owners. Since the credit union was moving into a new facility, it took the opportunity to design a new experience, one that wasn't hyper-focused on products. PACU studied the Universal model, a banking term used to explain how to employ one employee who can do a lot more. MEAs at PACU do everything now, which creates less hassle for the member. Members can also come behind the counter and see the same screen the teller sees, which is a huge deal. Members love it. When the pilot branch was opened, PACU closed another and lost nothing in the consolidation. It promoted the new experience and the branch grew much faster than before—partly because of the better location, but also because of the model and awareness. It did a lot more PR and saw more visitors from other banks and other areas. Members began helping other members and telling the story.

Finding the right hires (MEAs) was the biggest problem for PACU. People liked to talk about the building instead of the experience or values, and there was a lot of turnover with MEAs and management, which was frustrating.

In reflecting on the process, Tharpe wished she'd realized everything should be driven by results. "We could have been further along if we had paid attention to the results earlier," she said. "We want to create a social space and create an affinity and relationship with YPN (Young Professional Network). The next step is to build programs using their input." To that end, the credit union has a community event space, coffee bar, free Wi-Fi, and other amenities designed to draw the community in, differentiates itself from a bank, and helps members feel the credit union difference.

PACU's board was a part of the process, and Tharpe and her team spent a lot of time educating and teaching the board about the proposed changes, feeding them a lot of data supporting the reasons behind them. PACU gave the board a month to think about it and it made the recommendation several months later.

In terms of costs, the branch was pricier than a traditional branch, but everything else was about the same. Consolidation into a new building was ultimately an expense savings.

Moving forward, PACU is looking at ways to outsource non-core business competencies to free up resources and time for improving and building better member experiences.

PART 6

MOTIVATE

In this section, we cover the M in DREAM. Using a motivate structure to help demonstrate to members the value of their credit union ownership, along with the rest of the DREAM approach, will help your credit union differentiate itself from a crowded field and allow it to compete with FinTech startups.

21

SHOW YOUR MEMBERS THAT YOU AREN'T A BANK

Perhaps one of the more encouraging trends is that more and more credit unions are paying loyalty dividends. I believe this is an essential way to show members the credit union difference. By doing so, you motivate them to be loyal and believe in the credit union. The dollar amounts or types of rewards are less important than demonstrating to members that the credit union, as a cooperative, is different. A few years ago, 40 percent of credit unions planned to pay dividends each year, but only 10 percent actually did.

- Sixty percent of credit unions make a dividend decision based on the previous year—with net worth ratio, return on assets, and return on equity as top trigger points—versus including it in the annual budget.

- Ninety-one percent of credit unions use direct deposit to pay out their patronage dividends.
- Ninety percent of credit unions don't discuss paying a patronage dividend with their regulator prior to implementing the program.

One example of doing it right is Rogue Credit Union in Oregon, which pays out member loyalty dividends at the end of each year. That money is placed into a special savings account that earns a higher interest rate. (The member can't take that money out without losing the special interest rate.) RCU offers its members something unique, which rewards a certain behavior, and at the same time, it reinvests in its community. The credit union told members who received the rewards account that every time the member uses his or her credit card, Rogue would round up the change and place it into the member's loyalty dividend account. Now members are getting a constant feedback loop that something good is happening every time they complete a transaction.

As we look at all the different delivery channels credit unions offer, we need to examine and assess each interaction and ask, "How can I improve this experience to not just be table stakes, but to surprise and wow my member?"

Improving a member's experience doesn't have to be costly or fancy. Sometimes, it can be as simple as setting certain expectations and then over-delivering on them. For example, if you called into the call center and the automated voice told you the wait time was going to be three minutes, and then two seconds later someone greets you, you'd think that was awesome! These types of improvements can—and should—be implemented all over the place.

Another place to look is outside the industry at other cooperatives. My favorite example is REI. REI offers some great examples of things credit unions could do to convey the cooperative value proposition.

REI WAY	CU VERSION
Dividend back based on purchase value to buy more stuff	Dividend back used for a lower loan rate on new loans or a higher savings rate
Training and trips (experiences)	Bring in well-known financial experts for workshops. Have special clubs based on lifestyles: entrepreneur club, small business club, or first-time home buyer club, where you offer do-it-yourself remodel workshops.
Return policies (return anything for any reason)	Create more flexibility for loans or deposit mistakes members make. Make it super easy for members to trade in cars, or provide additional warranties for home repairs.
Garage sale (sell all the returned stuff at a twice-a-year early morning event)	Offer financial tune-ups twice a year at 7 a.m. on a Saturday for members to come in and take advantage of some special promotions. At the same time, auction off your repossessed cars to your members or sell them at a steep discount.
Make the member feel like they own the place	Make the member feel like they own the place

CASE STUDY: IDEAL CREDIT UNION

Credit unions are committed to quality member service and helping members achieve their financial and life goals. Like many other credit unions, Ideal evaluated its penetration among existing members and sensed additional opportunities to engage members and capture additional member wallet share. Ideal envisioned a member loyalty program in which they would provide upward scaling rewards as members used their products and services.

A key dependency for creating such a program was to seamlessly integrate multiple sources of data within the credit union and to provide a comprehensive picture of the members' products and how they use their products on a given day. Ideal was unable to successfully integrate the necessary data to run such a program until it partnered with OnApproach to integrate data from its core system along with other product databases using the OnApproach M360™ Analytics Platform.

The platform provided a reliable and validated single source for Ideal's transactional data, which enabled Ideal to have a member-centric view of its data and thereby make the VIP analytics app a reality.

Product Line	Data Source 1	Data Source 2	Data Source 3
Auto	X		
Certificates	X		
Checking	X		
Credit Cards			X
Home Equity	X	X	X
Money Market	X		
Mortgage	X	X	

What resulted was Ideal's new VIP rewards program, which included the following:

- **VIP Patronage Dividend.** Based on making at least 144 withdrawal transactions (debit card, ACH, ATM, etc.) from a consumer Ideal checking account within the calendar year.

- **VIP Loan Rebate Dividend.** Based on meeting VIP Patronage requirements and having two or more Ideal qualifying consumer loans that carried a balance in the calendar year.

The dividend amount is based on the sum of the monthly interest paid.

- **VIP Deposit Bonus Dividend.** Based on meeting VIP Patronage requirements and having one of three types of deposit accounts. The dividend is calculated by the average daily balance in qualifying accounts.

The VIP eligibility requirements are simple when viewed individually, but the combination of sixty-four distinct rules applied to ever-changing transactional data in the source systems made it a complex undertaking. Accuracy of information is critical. Members expect to receive the exact dividend amounts they have earned. Credit union management must be able to confidently use the ongoing information to evaluate the program to ensure the total payout falls within a budgeted amount. Ideal's data analytics platform (enabled by OnApproach) allowed them to automatically update a program with 15,000 qualifying members every day, with minimal ongoing maintenance.

Since 2012, Ideal Credit Union has been reaping the benefits of its VIP member loyalty program. Since the program's initiation, the program experienced greater than a 15% increase in the number of members receiving awards, totaling over 15,000 members. "VIP is one of the most popular member programs we've ever launched," Ideal CFO Dennis Bauer said. "Now, with the additional ability to drive other marketing programs with the VIP information, we are truly leveraging the value of our data." According to Dennis Bauer, "Our VIP program developed through M360 has helped in growing our product penetration to our membership. We have determined that the following four products drive profitability: Checking, Credit Card, Auto Loan, and Mortgage Loan. The VIP+ program is a primary reason why there has been a 20% increase in the last three years of the number of members with at least three of these products."

PART 7

———

BONUS SECTION: INNOVATE

22

WHAT SHOULD YOU STOP DOING?

If you've read this book this far, you're probably thinking, "Yikes! There's all these things to implement and change, and there's no way I can get all these things done! I'm scared to death that FinTechs are going to kick my butt and that the regulators are going to keep coming! How do I make sure I'm addressing all these things?"

What it comes down to is looking at what you can be best at and how you can differentiate from competitors. When you ask that question—what are we best at?—each board member, management team member, and CEO will have a different opinion based on their life stage and experience, so it's extremely difficult to reach consensus on what the credit union should be doing.

It often is easier to reach consensus on what the credit union *shouldn't* be doing.

I've seen credit unions outsource IT compliance, for example. IT compliance is certainly important, but it's not what a credit union should be known for. No one ever says, "My credit union has the best IT compliance! You should join!" The credit unions that outsourced it no longer owned any IT infrastructure and instead hired another entity to do it better. Other credit unions stop managing their own HR and outsource it to companies like a PEO (professional employer organization) agency. Some stop managing their ATMs. I've even seen some credit unions stop holding cash in branches, because it takes three or four employees to do so, which takes up a lot of time. Not having any cash in the branch frees up time for these employees to focus on other tasks and functions.

Another example: Tropical Credit Union hosted a "heroes" campaign several years ago that cost them $40,000. The campaign asked the community to nominate local heroes by submitting a video, and the credit union received 400 entries. From those entries, TCU invited community members to vote until they brought the hero pool down to ten candidates. TCU then reviewed that pool and picked a winner and a runner-up. The winner received $4,000, and the runner-up received $1,000. It was a highly successful promotion for the credit union, as it garnered a lot of publicity, earned the credit union community goodwill, and didn't cost too much. On top of that, TCU conducted everything online—no print ads—which saved it a bunch of money.

The following year, TCU decided to run the promotion again, but this time they wanted to expand the reach by spending more money promoting it through TV, radio, and print mailers. Not only did TCU increase its budget substantially, but the approach demanded a lot more work. Unfortunately, the expected return on investment wasn't as high as anticipated. The second year received the exact same amount of entries as the first year: 400, 85 percent of which were entered digitally!

Credit unions are stuck thinking statement stuffers, direct mail pieces, and so on are effective forms of reaching their membership, but in reality, they're not driving as much business as you think they are. What if you stopped doing them for three months? What would happen to your financials? We're better off moving away from traditional forms of marketing and communicating and spending more time and effort seeing what works digitally.

By focusing on what they're best at, some credit unions have done away with ATM machines. Instead, these credit unions instructed their membership to use any available ATM and told them they would refund any fees. Not only did this decision turn out to be more efficient and simpler to manage on the credit union's side, it also gave members the flexibility to use any ATM without worrying about wasting money on fees. These credit unions spent less money refunding members' fees than running, maintaining, and stocking an entire ATM network, so it ended up being a win-win.

Some credit unions have done away with branches altogether and instead focus their efforts on making their call centers fantastic. There are other entrants outside the market, like USAA, which don't have brick-and-mortar branches, so they're not spending any capital on that. Instead of spending a couple million dollars building a branch, they're spending that money building a better mobile app. The reallocation of the budget from a traditional brick-and-mortar setup is hugely impactful if you take advantage of the options technology offers. Two million dollars can build a hell of a mobile app compared to what you get out of building a physical branch. That mobile app will likely be used by 80 to 90 percent of your members, whereas a branch will likely be used by only 10 percent.

Another example—one of my favorites—is of LA Federal Credit Union, which stopped dealing with change—quarters, nickels, dimes, and pennies. Any transaction you complete, any check you deposit, any money you want to withdraw out of your account, LAFCU rounds up to a whole dollar and eats the difference. For example, if you deposit a check for $43.77, the credit union would deposit an even $44, eating the 23 cents. What a great experience for their members! They score a little extra money and it doesn't cost the credit union *that* much, saving it a ton of time not dealing with the hassle of change.

START DOING SOMETHING ELSE

With limited resources and unlimited wants—a basic economic problem—you have to stop doing something in order to do something else. The only way to get more of what we want is to do less of what we don't want. We hire a housekeeper to have more time with our family; we hire a gardener to take care of our landscaping so we can spend our time on something else. The people I pay to clean my house and mow my lawn are way more efficient than I am, since they have tools, better techniques, and better methodology—a worthwhile investment for the outcome.

If we can outsource actions in our personal lives, why don't we do more of that in our work lives? "My credit union can't be the best at human resources, so I'm going to find someone who's as good or better than I am at human resources and stop spending my brain power and capital on it." The same thing can be said in regards to infrastructure.

OUTSOURCING CREDIT AND DEBIT CARDS

A lot of credit unions use PSCU. PSCU is a credit card as well as a call center, and it manages balances and handles compliance issues related to credit cards. Through PSCU, credit unions offer a world-class experience, most of the time better than they could do on their own—not to mention one that's cheaper. The same thing can be said for COOP handling debit cards and ATMs. We're already accustomed as an industry to saying, "We can't be the best at managing our credit cards, so let's partner with PSCU. We can't be the best at managing our ATMs or our debit cards, so let's partner with COOP." We need to constantly be looking at functions we can't be the best at and say, "We don't need to be in those businesses."

CASE STUDY: DOL FEDERAL CREDIT UNION

Joan Moran, President and CEO of DOL Federal Credit Union, had a problem with payroll processing, especially in light of continuous staffing changes and turnover. "You can't mess up people's paychecks," Moran said. DOL previously outsourced health insurance and benefits and retained specific healthcare expertise, so it decided to outsource HR, since it lacked consistently high-caliber human resource professionals. In addition, continued payroll challenges were distracting the credit union from the core business at hand—helping members.

The credit union involved MDDCCUA in outsourcing HR, and first tried cross-training employees, but quickly discovered it needed services beyond payroll. In conjunction with outsourcing HR management, it outsourced its payroll processing. Right away, that was a significant improvement with an immediate impact. It greatly reduced the amount of time spent on time sheets, and also streamlined and forced a better process. "I wish we had thought of it sooner," Moran said. Even though the change was invisible to members, if DOL hadn't addressed the issue, it would have likely seen more turnover.

By outsourcing HR, DOL started focusing on member-facing marketing, sales, and technology.

CASE STUDY: WYHY
FEDERAL CREDIT UNION

Since October 2013, Bill Willingham, President and CEO of WyHy Federal Credit Union, has developed and reallocated technical resources so the credit union could focus on member-facing technology, specifically within the branch. The IT staff had bottlenecks, was spending tremendous time on compliance and infrastructure, and couldn't get to business technology problems. WyHy wanted to focus more time on growing wallet share and becoming more member-centric.

WyHy first outsourced core and compliance. "I wish we had moved to outsource core and infrastructure sooner," Willingham said. "The key to success was weekly meetings with key providers (MDT, OGO, COOP, PSCU, BA Group)." WyHy then outsourced marketing through the BA Group out of Minnesota, social media, website, data analytics, marketing campaigns, and media buys.

WyHy saw results quickly, starting with marketing. Five years into working with MDT on core system outsourcing, it saw a huge impact. (It took five years to fix the old code.) The credit union used to have three people supporting core, but outsourcing vendors forced best practices and policies, which led to better focus. It no longer needed to hire resources in a remote area and saw a much lower turnover. "I wish we had involved the vendor more in the process from the beginning, instead of trying to do it ourselves," Willingham said. "We ended up burning time trying to save some money, but ultimately it cost us money down the road. I also wish we would have done it sooner." Following outsourcing the core to MDT, WyHy outsourced IT infrastructure to Ongoing Operations and credit cards to PSCU.

WyHy's board was not a part of the process. The credit union basically presented the reasons why it needed to move in this direction and then started moving.

In terms of member benefits, WyHy's uptime is much better and things no longer go down. Moving forward, WyHy is looking to outsource accounting and consolidate the back office and collections.

23

BOARDS, CEOS, AND CIO ALIGNMENT STRATEGIES

A lot of credit unions struggle with finding alignment among their boards, management teams, CEOs, and CIOs. If you ask CEOs for a strategic plan, they come back with ten things they're working on. If you ask CIOs for their plan, they come back with twenty. If you look at both lists to see where they overlap, they usually don't, because CIOs are off focusing on trying to keep the lights on, spending 85 to 90 percent of their time patching, upgrading, and maintaining the infrastructure, while CEOs are making sure the credit union is delivering existing value propositions and trying to keep past decisions working for current members.

The first step is to take the credit union's strategic and IT plan and try to figure out how many things align: 70 to 80 percent should line up. If they don't, that's a red flag. Once you've looked over the two plans, approach the IT department or the CEO and ask, "Which of these things should we be doing and which can be outsourced?" Once you find that alignment, prioritize and start measuring the impact of spending time on those, adding in marketing automation, mobile wallet, a social media piece, and so on. The reality is most credit union CEOs, CIOs and marketing people don't know enough about content marketing or marketing automation to be able to lead those efforts.

Instead of trying to boil the ocean, ask yourself, "What are the universal skills we're going to need from IT and marketing?" The next level is, "What are the business processes necessary to deliver this different brand experience?" Measure those in member-facing technology, marketing automation, sales tools, technology, and data analytics—and pay attention to how you're improving.

Any business process improvement, training, or member-facing experience initiative that doesn't align with the priorities set by your team should be shelved for another time, if they're unlikely to positively impact the member experience.

EXERCISES

Imagine your credit union is two to three times larger than it is today. Try to look into the future and work backward. If it is a $1,000,000,000 credit union today, you'd imagine it to be $2,000,000,0000 tomorrow. What would your organization look like as a two-billion-dollar organization? How would you divide labor? What kind of branch infrastructure would you need? How would you be doing business tomorrow, and what kind of solutions, technology, infrastructure, and people would you need to be able to do that? Build a future org chart, then take your current org chart and compare the two. If you think it's going to take you seven years to reach two billion dollars, work backward year by year to where you are today. Make smaller changes without being too disruptive to your staff. Do the same for your infrastructure, and you'll have a nice evolution.

EXERCISE: BLANK SLATE

If you were to rebuild your credit union with a clean slate with everything you now know, what would it look like? Say you have one year to build a new organization with $500,000,000 in assets, 100 employees, and seven branches. What would you do today? What functions would you pick and choose? What would you stop doing? Which functions would add value? Build what that looks like, from org chart, physical infrastructure, technology planning, and similar perspectives. (You don't have to spend a ton of time on detail, but you need to build out those raw components.) Now you have a snapshot of how your ideal credit union would operate without any current baggage. You can then compare, contrast, and start implementing small changes to start working toward where you want to be.

EXERCISE: SYSTEM OF URGENCY

List all the things IT needs to do, and make a four-quadrant urgency system. You want an arrow on the left side that indicates escalating urgency and an arrow on the bottom going from left to right that indicates escalating importance. Take all the things IT is doing and after you plug them in, you should see one quadrant full of functions that are both urgent and important. That is where you should be spending a lot more of your time.

Ultimately, you want your board, management team, and CEO all aligned to say, "Here are the initiatives and how they will impact what the board is concerned about. Here's how we're delivering the branding, technology, and member-facing experience, and here are the CEO's responsibilities and IT's responsibility."

Here in an example of what that might look like:

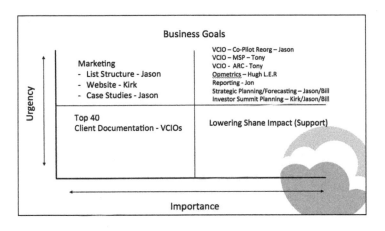

SHORT- VERSUS LONG-TERM

Be sure to break down any goals into sizable chunks quarter-by-quarter and year-by-year, so they don't become huge, unattainable tasks. Smaller weekly goals are more measurable and will lead to bigger progress the more time that passes. Even when you tackle something that might take three or five years to complete, make sure there are tangible goals you can track to show progress and that you are moving in the proper direction. Check off and eliminate items from each quadrant once they're completed, until your credit union is doing what it is best at.

24

CONCLUSION

___

The credit union industry is at a crossroads. With the continuous onslaught of regulation, an influx of agile FinTech solutions, and members who expect us to look like Zappos.com, credit unions can either adapt to the changing marketplace or fade into irrelevance. To adapt, we will need to shift our priorities to digital-first branding and offer the up-to-date and sophisticated technology our members now expect. We must leverage marketing automation, sales, social media, content marketing, branding, and member-facing technology to create and master our members' digital experience.

Credit unions on this path have started by working to align the management team, board, and CEO, so everyone is working toward the same goals. These credit unions have hired accordingly, appointing CMTOs (chief marketing technology officers) or heads of Retail Delivery to oversee critical digital channels. I also see these adaptive credit unions making the tough decisions to stop doing some things, so they can focus on functions that matter most to their business. While this roadmap may seem daunting, each step is small, and collectively they produce an outsize impact.

As you start thinking about internal alignment, go through the strategies, tools, and exercises in Chapter 23. At Ongoing Operations, we generally do one of those exercises every quarter; we would not attempt to do all of them in the same quarter. As I come across different business problems, I have found it helpful to have a good library of options to access to consider for each particular case.

While you are working on internal alignment, keep in mind that it's generally easier to find consensus on what you *can't* be best at than what you can. When you start the discussion of what your credit union can be best at, you'll likely hear a variety of answers. We can be the best at service. We can be the best at helping millennials. We can be the best at helping baby boomers. We can be the best at opening more branches in our community. We can be the best at giving away free popcorn. You get the idea.

When you start looking at the things you can't be best at, it's usually much easier to ask, "Are we going to be the best at running ATMs? Do we believe we're going to be better than a company that runs 50,000 ATMs?" Probably not. It's far easier to list a hundred things you're currently doing and identifying ten that you have no chance at ever being the best at. Find your strengths and focus on those. Find your greatest weaknesses and outsource them—or get rid of them altogether. You can expect some dissent. In my experience, it can be very difficult to reach consensus among boards, management, and CEOs on what the credit union can be best at. Everyone has their own perspective and opinions on what the credit union's strengths and weaknesses are, and there may be varying appetites for outsourcing.

By eradicating or outsourcing functions that aren't essential for delivering a strong digital experience, credit unions can then reallocate time and resources to learning, experimenting, testing, and deploying the various digital marketing tools used by FinTech competitors and delivering an amazing experience to members. The focus is to help members feel like proud owners by evangelizing the prime differentiator of credit unions—member ownership.

One of the ways to find help in outsourcing certain facets of doing business is to team up with other credit unions already doing it. I've seen groups of credit unions say, "None of us can be the best at collections. Let's all put some money in and hire a better collections person, who can really get the job done." I've seen this done with bulk purchasing supplies and sharing a CFO. There are various functionalities you can share with other credit unions that don't compete for your membership.

And the one thing about credit unions that hasn't changed—and shouldn't change—is that when we work together, we all win.

ACKNOWLEDGMENTS

All of the great people who helped me succeed in credit unions: Juri Valdov, Lindsay Alexander, Mimi Lieb (in memory), Joan Moran, Margie Click, Theresa Mann, William White, Kathy Geary, Dave Serlo (in memory), Jan Roche, Martin Breland, Bruno Sementilli, Mark Zook, Judy Sandberg, Guy Messick, Ray Crouse, Brian Lauer, Mark Zook, Paul Ablack, John Best, Chris Otey, Paul Fiore, Jeff Russell, Steve Salzer, Sarah Canepa-Bang, Kari Wilfong, Chip Filson, Mike Atkins, Rod Staatz, and many more.

ABOUT THE AUTHOR

———

A serial entrepreneur focused exclusively on credit-union technology, KIRK DRAKE has more than twenty years of experience designing and implementing advanced IT systems, solutions, and collaborations. Kirk started a high school bank at sixteen—before he knew about credit unions—and is the co-founder of CU Wallet, LLC and the founder of CUCTO; Ongoing Operations, LLC; and CU2.0 Strategist.

He served as chief technology officer for NIH Federal Credit Union, a $500 million financial institution, where he spearheaded critical system conversions to strategically advance the credit union, allowing it to better serve its members. As a leader in the industry, Kirk is adept at designing collaborative solutions and developing innovative technology platforms.

He is currently the chief executive of Ongoing Operations, which serves over 150 credit unions directly and over 1,000 indirectly. In 2010, Kirk teamed up with Paul Fiore, founder of Digital Insight, to create CU Wallet, a mobile wallet CUSO.

While not working, Kirk is an avid traveler, hiker, backpacker, husband, and father of three. He currently resides in southern Oregon, where he is helping his wife start a vineyard on a shoestring budget.